CELTIC
MYTHOLOGY
AND
RELIGION

DR. MACBAIN AND HIS STUDENTS.

CELTIC
MYTHOLOGY
AND
RELIGION

ALEXANDER MACBAIN

ORACLE

Celtic Mythology and Religion

First published in 1917 by Eneas Mackay, Stirling

This edition published in 1996 by Oracle Publishing Ltd.,
2A Kingsway, Royston, Hertfordshire,
SE8 5EG, England.

Copyright © this edition Oracle Publishing Ltd. 1996

ISBN 1 86196 008 5

Printed and bound in Guernsey by
The Guernsey Press Co. Ltd

CONTENTS.

LIST OF ILLUSTRATIONS.

INTRODUCTION.

ALEXANDER MACBAIN, generally and rightly regarded
as the greatest of our Scottish Celtic scholars, was
born in Glenfeshie, in Badenoch, on 22nd July, 1855,
and died on 3rd April, 1907, at Stirling. The ancestors of his father, John MacBain, were reputed
to hail from Lochaber. His mother was Margaret
Mackintosh, whose people were of the Mackintoshes
of Tirinie in Glen Tilt, descendants or connections
of the ancient *Tòiseach* of that ilk. In MacBain's
boyhood his district was so thoroughly Gaelic
speaking that at the age of eight or nine he knew
no English, while at fifteen his English was still
hesitating, and though he was quick to observe the
errors of others, he himself could not avoid similar
mistakes of grammar and idiom. He was bred in a
Gaelic atmosphere and in a district which in virtue
of its central position was full of the clan spirit and
clan traditions, an environment which influenced
him strongly throughout his life. In his early years,
he had his full share of the joys and the hardships
of the Highland lad of humble station, and more
than his share of the perfervid energy and deter-
mination which have raised so many such lads to
honour and fame. Some day the full story of
MacBain's early career may be given more completely
as related by himself in his *Journal,* a document of

great interest and value. " In the Introduction,"
he says, " I give all my early life up to the time I
commenced keeping a Journal, or the year 1870,
when the *Journal* proper commences ; and, moreover,
I also give an account of my ' ancestors ' in the said
Introduction." Here only a short sketch of these
early days can be given. He entered Insh School
on 25th November, 1863, and left it on 8th August,
1870. From December of 1870 till mid-April 1871,
he taught, quite alone, the school of Dunmullie,
Boat of Garten, which under him rose from twenty-
three to fifty-seven pupils. His salary consisted of
the fees. After this experience and some months of
attendance at Baldow School, where he began Greek,
he got work on the Ordnance Survey, first in Scotland, then in Wales. He had, however, no intention
of remaining permanently in the Survey; his aim
all along was, somehow or other, to work his way
to the University. His craving for knowledge of
every kind was intense ; his means of gratifying it
were slender; but he never lost an opportunity.
Before leaving Badenoch he had made good progress
in English, History, Latin and Mathematics, and had
contrived, by dint of purchase and borrowing, to
read a great deal of sound but exceedingly mis-
cellaneous literature. He had tried his hand at
poetry and had given it up. He had read astronomy
and done some architectural drawing, stirred thereto
by seeing the plans of some new buildings on the
Mackintosh estate. He had even tried painting. He

had the habit of taking stock from time to time of his attainments, his personal belongings, books, etc., and his physical development and appearance. He looked upon his little world with the same appraising, critical but kindly eye. He kept a full and careful note of his correspondence with his father, who had gone to better his fortune in America, and was deeply solicitous for his son's welfare. On the Ordnance Survey he added materially to his stock of knowledge and became expert in the operations of surveying, but in so far as his main purpose was concerned, the service was a failure, for he left it in 1873 as poor as when he entered it. He now studied for a short time at Baldow School, and succeeded in obtaining one of the Grammar School Bursaries provided under the scheme of the Reverend Dr. J. Calder Macphail. With this assistance, in autumn of 1874 he entered the Grammar School of Old Aberdeen, famous then, under the Rectorship of Dr. William Dey, as a preparatory school for Aberdeen University. Two years later he entered King's College as second Bursar, and could at last look forward with confidence to some realisation of his ambition. Here he is said to have impressed his fellow students as the ablest man of his year, a year which included James Adam, afterwards of Emmanuel College, Cambridge, foremost Platonist of his time. Though a good classical scholar, MacBain read for honours in philosophy, a subject which in after life he reckoned one of the most barren

of studies, and graduated in 1880. For a short time
he assisted Dr. Dey in the Grammar School ; thereafter, in 1880, he was appointed Rector of Raining's
School, Inverness, under the government of the
Highland Trust. He occupied this post till 1894,
when Raining's School was transferred to the Inverness Burgh School Board, and thereafter was officially
connected with the Secondary Department of the
Inverness High Public School. In 1901 his University of Aberdeen honoured him with the honorary
degree of LL.D. In 1905 Mr. Arthur J. Balfour,
then Prime Minister, in consideration of his great
services to Celtic, and specially Gaelic, philology,
history and literature, recommended him to the
King for a Civil List Pension of £90, as from 1st
April of that year. Two years later he died suddenly
in Stirling, where he had gone on business during
the Easter vacation.

As Headmaster of Raining's School, MacBain
succeeded in making his school occupy for the North
of Scotland a position similar to that held by the
Grammar School of Old Aberdeen under Dr. Dey.
His reputation attracted to it many of the ablest
lads from the whole Highland area. He taught
them to think for themselves, to insist on having
not only facts, but also, so far as in them lay, the
reasons why these things are so. Keen young men
were not slow to kindle at the master's quickening
fire. They gladly lived laborious nights and days,
doing with all their might that which was given

them to do. Raining's School became in those days a nursery of students who subsequently took the highest positions in the University classes, and became useful and distinguished men in their various callings. Some idea of the work is afforded by the fact that in MacBain's time the school, which began under him in 1880 with a secondary department of three, by 1890 had sent over one hundred to the Universities.

While thus actively and successfully engaged in the work of an arduous profession, MacBain was at the same time carrying on with extraordinary vigour those Celtic studies which won him a world-wide reputation. When he came to Inverness in 1880, the scientific study of Scottish Gaelic had already begun under Dr. Alexander Cameron of Brodick (ob. 1888), but little substantial progress had been made. In February of 1882, in his first speech at the annual dinner of the Gaelic Society of Inverness, MacBain said : " Hitherto the Highlanders have been too much inclined to guess, and too little inclined to accurate scientific research. We want a good critical edition of the Gaelic poets ; we want also a scientific Gaelic Dictionary dealing with the philology of the language." He was then twenty-seven, and was rapidly qualifying himself to deal with the philological requirements. On New Year's Day, 1875, being then a student at the Grammar School, he had written in his diary : " I think that I have now a good chance of yet appearing as an

M.A. on equal terms in education with the other literary men of our day, a goal which has always been my ambition to arrive at, that I may have confidence in discussing the topics which engross the attention of mankind. I dread to commit myself through ignorance, and ere I will appear (if ever I shall) in public, I will be backed up with a complete knowledge of the facts I speak on. This is high talking for a poor student in the second class of the Grammar School of Old Aberdeen." Here he enunciates a guiding principle from which he never swerved. He had ever the true scientific spirit in his respect for facts, and in the pains he took, and would have others take, in verifying them. No statement of his is made at haphazard. This reverence for truth he had the knack of inspiring in some, at least, of those who came in contact with him.

In Inverness he lived far from University centres and far from libraries. He made up for this partly by an expenditure on books which must have been out of proportion to his income, and partly by the direction he was able to give to the purchases of the local Free Library, as a result of which its reference department is exceedingly complete and useful on the historical side. Inverness itself was at that time rich in men of native talent and literary instincts. In particular the Gaelic Society, founded in 1871, by the discussions at its meetings and by the field for publication offered by its *Transactions*, exercised

an important influence. There MacBain found
companionship that was much to his taste ; he
attended the meetings regularly, and contributed
eighteen valuable papers to its *Transactions*, the
first of which was that on *Celtic Mythology* read on
23rd February, 1883. Of the others, some of the
most important are his edition of the *Book of Deer*
(volume xi.) ; *Badenoch History, Clans and Place
Names* (vol. xvi.) ; *Ptolemy's Geography* (xviii.) ; the
last of which he himself considered " the best thing
he had done ; " the *Norse Element in Highland Place
Names* (xix.) ; *Early Highland Personal Names*
(xxii) ; *Place Names of Inverness-shire* (xxv.).
In addition, he wrote the introductions to volumes
x.-xxv. of the Society's *Transactions*, constituting
a history of Gaelic literature and of the Gaelic move-
ment for the period covered by them. To the
Transactions of the Inverness *Scientific Society and
Field Club* he contributed papers on *Celtic Burial*
(vol. iii.) ; *Who were the Picts?* (vol. iv.) ; *The
Chieftainship of Clan Chattan* (vol. v.). He wrote
many articles and reviews for the local newspapers.
In addition to all this MacBain became, in 1886,
editor of the *Celtic Magazine*, and was also for five
years joint editor of the *Highland Monthly*. All
MacBain's articles show how firmly he held to his
guiding principle, verified knowledge of the facts.

In 1892, in conjunction with his lifelong friend,
the Rev. John Kennedy, Caticol, Arran, a Badenoch
man, MacBain published *Reliquiae Celticae* (two

volumes), being the literary remains of the Rev.
Dr. Alexander Cameron, Brodick, also a native of
Badenoch. In connection with this undertaking, he
completed and printed the transcription of the
Fernaig MS., which Cameron had not lived to
finish. His *Etymological Gaelic Dictionary* appeared
in 1896. On this, of course, he had spent much
time ; in his usual manner, he both mastered the
principles and made himself acquainted with all
that had been done by scholars, British, French,
German and Italian. The *Dictionary* was his crowning achievement, and was at once recognised as
marking an era in Celtic Philology. A second edition,
which he did not live to superintend, was published
by Mr. Eneas Mackay, Stirling, in 1911. In 1902 he
edited Skene's *Highlanders of Scotland*, with valuable
and characteristic but all too brief notes. In the
same year, in conjunction with Mr. John Whyte,
he edited *MacEachen's Gaelic Dictionary*, a most
useful work. Along with Mr. Whyte he also brought
out *How to Learn Gaelic*, with a brief but scientific
outline of Gaelic grammar. This handbook is now
in its fourth edition.

The bare statement of MacBain's achievement in
respect of output marks him as possessing extraordinary power of application. Yet it would be a
complete mistake to regard him as a student only.
He was a full-blooded man, with a keen enjoyment
of life, and, it is only fair to say, with a distinctly
Bohemian temperament. His leisure for social inter-

course was small ; but he had his own circle of
intimates, which for many years met weekly in a
spirit of good fellowship reminiscent at once of the
old London coffee-house days and of the Highland
céilidh. In congenial company, MacBain became
discursive, humorous, satirical, charming in manner
and personality, with the power of making others
feel at their best. Argument he disliked, especially
on matters within his own domain, whence he was
sometimes accused of " dogmatism." His dogmatism, however, was that of a man who has based his
opinion on a wide induction and knows what is
meant by proof, but on the other hand does not
choose always to rehearse the process by which his
judgment has been arrived at, especially to such as,
in any case, would not appreciate that process. No
man could be more generous in helping others.
Either by letter or by conversation, the stores of his
knowledge were open to all fellow-students. Of
jealousy he was wholly free : his one aim was to
add to the sum total of scientific knowledge, to
enlarge the kingdom of facts. Sometimes his gener-
osity was poorly rewarded ; this, knowing human
nature, he took philosophically. He had the power
characteristic of great minds of getting straight to
the essentials of a question, and of seeing things in
true perspective. He had the insight of the philo-
sopher into the significance of the facts he dealt
with, and the consequent power to correlate and
illumine them. His mind was powerfully analytic,

and in nearly, if not quite, as high a degree synthetic.
As a critic, while highly appreciative of good work.
he was not lenient to error, especially if the error
arose from negligence in verifying facts that ought
to have been verified. Charlatans found to their
cost that he could wield a grievous cudgel. But he
was fair in statement, and with native courtesy
and nobility of heart he was ready to recognise
the good points even of a weakling. His reputation
among scholars all over Europe was very high, as I
have occasion to know from appreciations of his work
by practically all the leading Celtists of his day in
connection with his Civil List pension. In his later
years, though his brain was active and his interest
unabated, he no longer possessed the physical
elasticity necessary to continue the strain to which
he had subjected himself. From his youth upwards
he had lived a full and hard life, and had indeed
overtaxed a strong constitution. MacBain had
more than achieved the ambitions of his boyhood.
The poor struggling Badenoch lad had taken his
place among the scholars of Europe ; he had won
the highest academic distinction and national
recognition. His premature death was a disaster
which to those who knew him well was full of pathos.
The portrait which appears at the beginning of this
book represents him in his prime. My own recol-
lection of him may be quoted from an article in the
Celtic Review written a few days after his death :
" And now he is gone, and Inverness is a less interest-

ing place than it was. The sturdy, square figure,
the massive head, the rugged, kindly face, the shrewd
grey eyes twinkling under bushy brows, are now but
memories. We shall miss his sage counsel and his
friendly clasp; we shall long in vain for the light
and leading that he alone could give in many departments. He was a great man, and he deserved well
of Scotland. We shall not look upon his like again."

The value of Dr. MacBain's work can be best
appreciated by considering the condition in which
Gaelic scholarship would now be without it. His
researches and original contributions as embodied
in his Dictionary have raised Gaelic philology to
the highest scientific level, and—a service of equal
importance—have brought the whole subject into
convenient and accessible form for the student.
Some misconceptions as to its design and scope are
dealt with by MacBain himself in a prefatory note
to *Further Gaelic Words and Etymologies* in volume
xxi. of the Gaelic Society's *Transactions* (incorporated
in the second edition). "Nor did the work fail to
meet with critics who acted on Goldsmith's golden
rule in the *Citizen of the World*—to ask of any comedy
why it was not a tragedy, and of any tragedy why
it was not a comedy. I was asked how I had not
given derivative words, though for that matter most
of the seven thousand words in the Dictionary are
derivatives; such a question overlooked the character of the work. Manifest derivatives belong to
ordinary dictionaries, not to an etymological one.

This was clearly indicated in the preface. . . . Another criticism was unscientific in the extreme. I was found fault with for excluding Irish words ! Why, it was the best service I could render to Celtic philology, to present a pure vocabulary of the Scottish dialect of Gaelic." As a matter of fact, the Dictionary is remarkably complete within the limits assigned to it. Its conclusions will, as a rule, remain firm, for they are based on facts, and they can be criticised to any purpose only by experts of experience. For the ordinary student the wisest course is to try to understand the principles on which the conclusions are based.

In the application of the principles of scientific philology to the two special departments of names of places and personal names, Dr. MacBain was, so far as Scotland is concerned, a pioneer. In dealing with Norse names as they appear now after many centuries of use in the mouths of Gaelic speakers, he came to realise what had not been realised previously, namely, that such changes as take place between Norse and Gaelic do not occur at haphazard, but are on the whole regular and capable of being stated in detail. Certain changes are invariable ; others vary according to district ; others are impossible. It follows that the value of any proposed interpretation depends in the first instance on the accuracy with which the true pronunciation of the name in Gaelic has been ascertained. Additional data, often of value, may of course, be got from charters, etc., but the genuine Gaelic pronunciation comes first. In dealing with Celtic names, the same principle holds. Success depends on accurate data, interpreted in the light of a historical knowledge of the language and its laws of sound. In all MacBain's work these principles are operative, and it is this fact that makes his work a model.

Practically all our knowledge of Highland personal names is due to Dr. MacBain's researches, as set forth in the Inverness Gaelic Society's *Transactions* and in the *Celtic Review*, volume ii. These papers, however, represent but a part of his industry and of his knowledge of the subject. He has left MS. collections from charter sources, etc., bearing on a vast number of Highland personal names, and forming a valuable basis of interpretation, but he himself did not commit the interpretation to paper.

With regard to the Pictish question, Dr. MacBain argued with much force on the one hand against Skene's view that the language of the Picts was really Gaelic and on the other against the view expressed by Professor Rhys that the Pictish language was non-Aryan. MacBain's statement of the case will be found in his papers (1) on *Ptolemy's Geography ;* (2) *Who Were the Picts ?* (Inverness Field Club *Transactions*, vol. iv.) ; (3) *The Ethnology of Celtic Scotland* in his edition of Skene's *Highlanders*, pages 381-401. In his view the Picts were racially mixed, and linguistically Celtic, and the form of Celtic spoken by them was of the Brettonic or Cymric branch, that is, Old Welsh, not Old Gaelic. With these views most scholars now agree.

The present volume contains three of his earlier essays. The essay on *Celtic Mythology* was his first contribution to the *Transactions* of the Gaelic Society, and while it is interesting historically and contains much valuable matter, both its general attitude and its conclusions have to be considered in the light of subsequent researches, especially Sir J. G. Frazer's *Golden Bough*. Of this Dr. MacBain himself was well aware, and he had, in point of fact, largely ceased to hold by the theories which were in favour at the date when the essay was written. In justice to MacBain, this qualification has to be kept in view. No such qualification attaches to the other two essays, *The Druid Circles*, and *Celtic Burial*. False ideas about the Druids he considered, rightly, to be the source of much vain and erroneous speculation, and in this respect he was wont to speak of them, together with the Culdees and the Picts of Galloway, as the " three frauds " of Scoto-Celtic history. The essay on *Celtic Burial* is another token of the keen interest taken by MacBain in the archaeological side of Celtic studies.

The publication of these essays will, it is hoped, be welcomed by many. There is among MacBain's papers abundant material for several further volumes.

WILLIAM J. WATSON.

EDINBURGH,
May, 1916.

CELTIC MYTHOLOGY AND RELIGION.

This work was first published in the " Celtic Magazine" in 1883-4.
First published in book form, 1885.

CELTIC MYTHOLOGY

AND RELIGION

THE field of Mythology, strictly defined, embraces the fabulous events believed in by a nation and the religious doctrines implied in these. But the term is for convenience' sake extended so as to include the kindred subject of folk-lore. Now folk-lore includes all those popular stories of which the fairy tales of our nursery are a good illustration, and where the religious element implied in Mythology is absent. The term Celtic Mythology, in these papers, is understood, therefore, to include the popular traditions and legendary tales of the Celts, the fabulous actions and exploits of their heroes and deities, the traditions of their early migrations, their fairy tales, and the popular beliefs in regard to the supernatural world. The scope of the discussion will include an introductory section or two on the general principles of Mythology—its cause and spread, and the connection of the Mythology of the Celts with those of the kindred nations of Europe and Asia.

CHARACTER OF MYTH.

" There was once a farmer, and he had three daughters. They were washing clothes at a river. A hoodie crow came round, and he said to the eldest one, ' '*M-pos-u-mi*—Will you marry me—farmer's daughter ? ' ' I won't, indeed, you ugly brute ; an ugly brute is a hoodie,' said she. He came to the second one on the morrow, and he said to her, ' '*M-pos-u-mi*—Wilt thou wed me ? ' ' Not I, indeed,' said she ; ' an ugly brute is a hoodie.' The third day he said to the youngest, ' '*M-pos-u-mi*—Wilt thou wed me—farmer's daughter ? ' ' I will wed thee,' said she ; ' a pretty creature is the hoodie.' And on the morrow they married.

" The hoodie said to her, ' Whether wouldst thou rather that I should be a hoodie by day and a man at night ; or be a hoodie at night and a man by day ? ' ' I would rather that thou wert a man by day and a hoodie at night,' says she. After this he was a splendid fellow by day and a hoodie at night. A few days after he got married he took her to his own house.

" At the birth of the first child, there came at night the very finest music that ever was heard about the house. Every one slept, and the child was taken away. Her father came to the door in the morning, and he was both sorrowful and wrathful that the child was taken away.

" The same thing, despite their watching, happened at the birth of the second child : music—sleep—and stealing of the child. The same thing happened, too, at the birth of the third child, but on the morning of the next day they went to another house that they had, himself and his wife and his sisters-in-law. He said to them by the way, ' See that you have not forgotten something.' The wife said, ' I forgot my coarse comb.' The coach in which they were fell a withered faggot, and he flew away as a hoodie !

" Her two sisters returned, and she followed after him. When he would be on a hill-top, she would follow to try and catch him ; and when she would reach the top of a hill, he would be in the hollow on the other side. When night came, and she was tired, she had no place of rest or dwelling. She saw a little house of light far from her, and though far from her, she was not long in reaching it.

" When she reached the house she stood deserted at the door. She saw a little laddie about the house, and she yearned after him exceedingly. The housewife told her to come in, that she knew her cheer and travel. She lay down, and no sooner did the day come than she rose. She went out, and as she was going from hill to hill, saw a hoodie, whom she followed as on the day before. She came to a second house ; saw a second laddie ; pursued the hoodie on a third day, and arrived at night at a third house. Here she was told she must not sleep, but be clever and catch the hoodie when he would visit her during night. But she slept ; he came where she was, and let fall a ring on her right hand. Now, when she woke, she tried to catch hold of him, and she caught a feather of his wing. He left the feather with her, and went away. In the morning she did not know what to do till the house-wife told her that he had gone over a hill of poison, over which she could not go without horse shoes on her hands and feet. She gave her man's clothes, and told her to learn smithying till she could make horse shoes for herself.

" This she did, and got over the hill of poison. But on the day of her arrival, she found that her husband was to be married to the daughter of a great gentleman that was in the town. As festivities were in progress, the cook of the house asked the stranger to take his place and make the wedding meal. She watched the bridegroom, and let fall the ring and feather in the broth intended for him. With the first spoon he took up the ring, with the next the feather. He asked for the person who cooked the meal, and said, ' that now was his married wife.' The spells went off him. They turned back over the hill of poison, she throwing the horse shoes behind her to him, as she went a bit forward, and he following her. They went to the three houses where she had been. These were the houses of his three sisters ; and they took with them their three sons, and they came home to their own home, and they were happy." *

*Abridged from Campbell's West Highland Tales, vol. i, p. 63.

Such is a good specimen of the folk-tale, and the folk-tales are merely the modern representatives of the old Mythology—merely the detritus, as it were, of the old myths which dealt with the gods and the heroes of the race. In the above tale we are in quite a different world from the practical and scientific views of the 19th century ; we have birds speaking and acting as rational beings, and yet exciting no wonder to the human beings they come in contact with ; supernatural spells whereby men may be turned into animals ; a marriage with a bird, which partially breaks these spells, and the bird becomes a man for part of the day ; supernatural kidnapping, ending in the disappearance of the man-bird ; and pursuit of him by the wife through fairy regions of charms and spells and untold hardships—a pursuit which ends successfully. It looks all a wild maze of childish nonsense, unworthy of a moment's serious consideration ; it would certainly appear to be a hopeless subject for scientific research ; for what could science, whose object is truth, have to do with a tissue of absurdities and falsehoods ? But this view is a superficial one, though it is the one commonly held. On looking more deeply into the matter, we shall find that after all there is a method in the madness of Mythology, and that the incongruous mass of tales and broken-down myths that make up a nation's folk-lore is susceptible of scientific treatment. Science first attacks the problem by the method of comparison ; it compares

the myths and tales of one nation with those of another, with the view of discovering similarities.
The outlines, for example, of the tale already given,
exist not merely in one or two more tales in our own
folk-lore, but can also be traced over all the continent
of Europe, as well as in many parts of Asia. The
outline of the tale is this—The youngest and best
of three daughters is married or given up to some
unsightly being or monster, who in reality is a most
beautiful youth, but who is under certain spells
to remain in a low form of life until some maiden
is found to marry him. He then regains his natural
form, though, as a rule, only partially; and the
newly-married pair have to work out his complete
redemption from the spells. But, just as he is about
to be free from the spells, the curiosity or disobedience
of the wife ruins everything; he disappears, and then
follows for the wife the dark period of wandering
and toil, which can be brought to an end only by
the achievement of tasks, generally three in number,
each hopelessly beyond human powers. The husband, who meanwhile has forgotten, owing to the
nature of the spells upon him, all about his wife,
is on the eve of marrying another, when the last
task of all is accomplished by the persevering courage
of the wife. The spells then leave him for ever, and
happiness reigns in the household ever after.

There are in our Highland folk-lore one or two
versions of this same tale. The story of the " Daughter of the Skies," in Mr. Campbell's book, is one

variation. Here the hoodie crow is replaced by a
little doggie, and the wife's disobedience is clearly
brought out, while the supernatural machinery—
the magical scissors and needle, for example—is
much more elaborate. The tale also is found in
Norway ; in the Norse tale, " East of the Sun and
West of the Moon," the hero appears at first as a
white bear, who, on his marriage with the heroine,
becomes a man by night. She must not, however,
see him, for light must not fall on his body or else
he at once disappears. But the wife, instigated
by her mother, steals a sight of him by lamp-light,
with the consequence that he awakes and vanishes.
Then follow her trials, pursuit, and recovery of him.
The beautiful Greek tale of Psyche and Cupid is but
a variation of the same myth. Psyche, the youngest
of three royal daughters, incurs the wrath of Venus,
who sends Cupid to inspire her with love for something contemptible ; as Titania, in Shakespeare,
is made to fall in love with the transformed weaver,
Bottom. But Cupid, captivated by her beauty,
falls in love with her himself, conveys her to a secret
cave, and visits her only at night, under strict charge
of her not attempting to see him by any light. Her
jealous sisters persuade her that she is married to
some ugly monster, and she accordingly determines
to disobey his injunctions, and inspect him by lamp-
light. In so doing, she allows in her admiration
of his beauty, a drop of hot oil to fall on his shoulder,
and he awakes, and escapes. She suffers woes

untold in her pursuit of him, being finally a slave
in the household of Venus, who treats her very cruelly.
But, of course, she recovers her lost lover at long
last. And, again, in India, in the old religious
books of the Brahmins, is a somewhat similar tale—
the story of Urvasi and Pururavas, the main features
of which are the same as the Gaelic and Greek tales
already given. To the English reader, the well-
known tale of " Beauty and the Beast " will at
once occur as an exact parallel to all these. And,
if we take the myths where the heroine is the loathly
monster, we shall find an equally wide distribution.
We have the Hindu tale, where the Princess is dis-
guised as a withered old woman; the Loathly
Lady of Teutonic Mythology; and the Celtic story
of Diarmad's love for the daughter of the king of
the Land under the Waves, who appears first as a
hideous monster, and becomes, on approaching
Diarmad, the most beautiful woman ever seen.

Thus, then, we have traced the same myth among
nations so widely apart as the Celts and Hindus,
while, intermediate between these, we found it among
the Greeks and Teutons. And some myths are
even more widely distributed than that; the tale of
the imprisoned maiden and the hero who rescues
her from the dragon or monster appears among all
the nations of Europe as well as among many of the
nations of Asia. Hence, from India in the East,
to Ireland in the West, we may find a great mass of
mythical tales common to the various nations.

And this being the case, it may plainly become a matter of scientific enquiry, first, What the cause of these peculiar myths and tales can be ? and, secondly, What the significance is of their wide distribution ?

CAUSE OF MYTH.

The cause and origin of these myths have puzzled philosophers of all ages, and it is only a generation ago when the first unravelling of the difficult problem really took place. In olden times their origin was set down to the well-known faculty of invention that man possesses ; they were mere inventions and fictions, mostly purposeless, though some were evidently intended for explanations of natural phenomena or of historical events, and others again for the conveyance of moral truth. There were practically two schools of myth-explainers ; those who regarded myths as mere allegories or parables, and from them extracted codes of moral obligation and hidden knowledge of the mysteries of nature ; and, again, those who, so to speak, " rationalised " the myths—that is to say, those who explained myths as exaggerated real events. Some of these explained, for example, Jupiter as king of Crete in the pre-historic times ; and, again, the giant that Jack killed, according to such explanations, was not necessarily far exceeding the natural limits of six or seven feet in height, for the only point to notice was that he was a big burly brute of little sense, overcome by the astuteness of a much lesser man. But this theory gets into grave difficulties when it grapples with the supernatural and the supranatural ; in fact, it fails ignominiously. And as to the allegorical theory, while it has no difficulty in explaining Jack the Giant Killer as merely the personification of the truth that power of mind is superior to power of body, that theory is completely wrecked in explaining the myths of Jupiter and the gods generally. No allegory can explain most of these myths, especially the older myths ; while the different explanations given by different " allegorizers " of even the simplest myths point to a fundamental error in this theory. Now, it must not be supposed that both allegory and real events had no share in the formation of myths ; they were, indeed, most potent factors in the later stages of Mythology, and must have existed all along as a cause for myth. Another theory may be noticed in passing as to the origin of myths in regard to the deities and cosmogony of the world. It may be called the " degradation " theory, and the principle of it is this : As all languages were supposed by theologians to be descendants of the original Hebrew tongue spoken in Eden, so the Mythology of all nations must be more or less a broken-down remembrance of the Hebrew religion and philosophy, first imparted to man in the Garden of Eden. The

stoutest supporter of this view is Mr. Gladstone.
He goes so far as to hold that distinct traces of the
Trinity can be found in Greek Mythology, and he
consequently resolves Zeus, Appollo, and Athena
into the three persons of the Trinity ! Supposing
for a moment that this theory of the degradation
of myth was true, or, indeed, that our only explanation was either or both of the other theories, what a
mass of senseless wickedness and immorality much
of the deservedly admired Greek Mythology would
be ? Such theories would argue equal wickedness
in the race from whose fancy such inventions sprung :
for the Greek Olympus is very full of rapine, paricide,
and vice. Yet the Greeks were neither an immoral
nor degraded race, but far otherwise. It is this
dark side of a nation's Mythology that has puzzled
and shocked so many philosophers and made ship-
wreck of their theories as to the origin of myths.

With the rise of the science of language and its
marked success, all within this century, a complete
revolution has taken place, not merely in the case
of philology itself, but also in the kindred subjects
of Ethnology and Mythology. The methods adopted
in linguistic research have also been adopted in the
case of Mythology—first, all preconceptions and
national prejudices have been put aside ; then a
careful, even painful examination and comparison
of languages have been made, to find laws of inter-
change of sounds ; a consequent discovery of the
relationships between languages has taken place ;

and lastly, a discussion as to the origin of language
is thus rendered possible.   Exactly the same methods
have been employed in the elucidation of myths,
with a success that, on the whole, is gratifying.
In so airy and fanciful a subject, results of such strict
scientific accuracy cannot be obtained as in the
kindred science of language.   And a good deal of
harm has also been done, even with scientific methods,
by pressing some theories of explanation too far.
Some Mythologists, for example, are too apt to
reduce every myth to a myth about the sun, and
hence the evil repute of the " solar myth " theory.
But this is merely a good theory injudiciously used ;
it does not alter the fact of the importance in
Mythology of the sun worship.

The theory of the cause of myth that finds most
favour at the present time is that which explains
myth in connection with, and dependence on, language ; while at the same time due regard is had to
the other possible sources of it in allegory, analogy,
and real, though exaggerated, events.   The way
in which language gives rise to myth can, however,
be understood only after a consideration of the
mental powers, state of culture, and consequent
interpretation of nature which existed among primitive and myth-making men.   Language is but the
physical side, as it were, of mythology, and the
mental side of it must be considered before the action
of language can be appreciated properly.   The origin
of myth springs from the same cause as the origin

of science ; they are both man's attempt to interpret his surroundings. Myth is but the badly remembered interpretation of nature given in the youth and inexperience of the world when the feelings were predominant ; science is the same interpretation in the old age of the world, given under the influence of the " freezing reason's colder part." Man in the myth-making stage was ignorant of the cause and real character of the mighty natural forces around him—ignorant even of the unaltering uniformity of nature—indeed the only thing the Celts said they were afraid of was that the heavens should fall ! The relations of cause and effect they interpreted by their own feelings and will-power ; every moving thing, animate or inanimate, was regarded as impelled by a force akin to that which impelled man ; that is, by a will-force. Even stationary nature— the everlasting hills and the solid earth—was endowed with feeling, will, and thought. All the mental powers that man found controlling his own actions were unconsciously transferred to nature. A personal life was accordingly attributed to sun, moon, clouds, winds, and the other natural powers ; they were looked upon as performing their special functions by means of faculties of mind and body analogous to those of man or beast. The varying phenomena of the sky, morn and eve, noon and black-clouded night, were the product of the life that dwelt in each. The eclipse of the sun, for example— a most dreaded event in ancient times—was supposed to be caused by a wild beast attempting to swallow the lord of day ; and men poured forth, as some savages do yet, with timbrels and drums, to frighten away the monster. The clouds were cows with swelling udders, milked by the sun and wind of heaven—the cattle of the sun under the care of the wind. The thunder was the roar of a mighty beast ; the lightning, a serpent darting at its prey. Modern savages are in much this state of culture, and their beliefs have helped greatly in unravelling the problem of mythology. The ideas which children form of outward nature exemplifies in some degree the mythic age through which the race in its childhood passed. " To a little child not only are all living creatures endowed with human intelligence, but everything is alive. In his world, pussy takes rank with ' Pa ' and ' Ma ' in point of intelligence. He beats the chairs against which he has knocked his head ; the fire that burns his finger is ' naughty fire ; ' and the stars that shine through his bedroom window are eyes like mamma's, or pussy's, only brighter."

It was on these wrong impressions—this anthropomorphic view of nature—that language was founded. Language, in man's passing to a higher state of culture, still kept, stereotyped and fixed, the old personal explanations and statements about nature ; the language did not change, but man's views of natural causes and events changed very much as he got more civilised—more free from the influence of his feelings, and more under the sway of his reasoning powers. The knowledge and ideas of earlier men were thus, as it were, fossilised in language, and when the feeling and personification impressed on language had passed into a more intellectual age, the result was misinterpretation and a too literal acceptance of many of the warm and vivid epithets employed of old. The personal explanation of the sun's motion, for instance, and the attributes and epithets given to it, all charged with life and feeling, were in the course of time and language taken in a more literal way, and, since slightly more scientific views were held as to the real nature of the sun, the old explanations were fastened to a separate sun-god, and thus a divorce was made between the sun and the personality given to it in the old epithets and explanations. The result was that there came to be a sun and a sun-god, Apollo, quite separate ; and the history given to this sun-god was taken from the life explanations formerly given, in personal and anthropomorphic language, of the sun's daily and yearly course, his " rising " and " setting," for example, expressions which, though anthropomorphic, are still in use. A myth cannot, therefore, well arise unless the true meaning of a word or phrase has been forgotten and a false meaning or explanation fastened on it. We may take an example from Greek mythology to illustrate this. Prometheus, the fire-bringer, is merely the personification of the wooden fire-drill ; for the word is derived from the same

source as the Sanscrit pramanthas,   the " fire
machine." Transplanted to Greek soil, the word
lost its original signification with the loss of the
thing signified, and became a mythological name,
for which a new etymology had to be coined.   Now,
" promethes," in Greek, means " provident," and
so Prometheus, the fire-bringer, was transformed
into the wise representative of forethought, who
stole the fire from heaven for suffering humanity ;
and a brother was supplied him in the foolish
Epimetheus or " afterthought."   And thereby hangs
one of the most famous and noble myths of antiquity.

Gaelic, in its modern shape even, presents some
very startling personifications of natural objects.
The regular expression for " The sun is setting "
is " Tha a' ghrian 'dol a laidhe "—" going to bed."
Mr. Campbell, in his very literal and picturesque
translation of the West Highland tales, does not
hesitate to follow the Gaelic even in its most personal
metaphors. " Beul na h-oidhche," " nightfall,"
is given literally as " the mouth of night."   Gaelic
poetry, too, is as a rule much more instinct with life
and feeling in dealing with natural objects than
English poetry. Ossian's address to the setting
sun may be quoted to show what a mine of metaphor,
and consequent mythology, exists in our poetic
and elevated language—

> " An d' fhàg thu gorm astar nan speur,
> A mhic gun bheud, a's òr-bhuidh' ciabh ?
> Tha dorsan na h-oidhche dhuit rèidh,
> Agus pàilliun do chlos 'san iar.

Ihig na stuaidh mu'n cuairt gu mall
A choimhead fir a's glaine gruaidh,
A' togail fo eagal an ceann
Ri d' fhaicinn cho àillidh 'nad shuain.
Gabhsa cadal ann ad chòs,
A ghrian, is till o d' chlos le aoibhneas."

These lines bring us back to the anthropomorphism of the Vedic hymns of India, to which alone, in their richness of personification and mythic power, they can be compared.

Allied to the linguistic theory of myth is also the simpler case of those myths consciously started to explain the names of nations, countries, and places. A common method of accounting for a national name was to invent an ancestor or patriarch who bore that name in an individual form. Britain, so say the myths, is so named from Brutus, grandson of Æneas, the Trojan hero, who first ruled here. Scotland gets its name from Scota, the daughter of Pharaoh. The names of places are dealt with in the same way, and, if the name is anyway significant, the myth takes the lines indicated by the popular etymology of the name. This is the origin of the name of Loch-Ness: "Where Loch-Ness now is there was once a fine glen. A woman went one day to the well to fetch water, and the spring flowed so much that she got frightened, left her pitcher, and ran for her life. Getting to the top of a hill, she turned about and saw the glen filled with water. 'Aha!' said she, 'tha loch ann a nis;' and hence the lake was called Loch-Ness."

A somewhat similar account is given of the origin
and name of Loch-Neagh, in Ireland, and Loch-Awe,
in Argyleshire.

From such myths as the last we gradually pass to
myths that do not depend in the least on the
quibbling and changes of language, but are, consciously or unconsciously, forged explanations of
national customs, historical events, or natural
phenomena. Thus the custom among the Picts
whereby the succession was in the female line, was
mythically explained by Bede, thus : The Picts,
having invaded Scotland, came to terms with the
indigenous Gaels, and, as they brought no women
with them, the compact was that, if the Gaels
gave them their daughters as wives, the succession
would be in the female line. Again, has the reader
ever thought why the sea is salt ? Well, this is the
reason why. A man once got possession, it is needless to detail how, of a fairy quern which was " good
to grind anything," only requiring certain cabalistic
words to set it going or to stop it. A ship captain
bought it to grind salt for him on his voyage. In
mid-ocean the captain gave the quern the necessary
order to grind salt, and it did ; but unfortunately
he forgot the incantation for stopping it. The
quern ground on and filled the ship with salt till
it sank to the bottom of the sea, where the quern
is still grinding salt. And that is the reason why
the sea is salt. If any one is sceptical, just let him
taste the sea water and he will know its truth !

SPREAD OF MYTH.

Closely akin to the consideration of the cause of myth is the question why myths and tales, evidently of the same origin, exist among nations differing widely both in language and locality. We found that tales of transformed lovers, descending even to similarities in minute details, and hence showing evidences of a common source, existed among all the chief nations of Europe, Western Asia, and India. Besides, other myths of a more general character are found all over the world. Now, what is the cause of this wide distribution of the same myths ? Two or three explanations are offered for this, each of which can correctly explain why some particular myths or tales are, but none of which can explain why the whole body of mythology and folk-lore is, so widely distributed. Some hold that the stories and myths have been borrowed or trans-mitted from one nation to another ; travellers and translators, they think, will account for nearly the whole of them. While it cannot be denied that many tales have permeated from one nation to another, this will by no means account for the similarities of myths among two nations or more, in whose language and customs these myths are so deeply embedded and ingrooved that we should have to say the language too was borrowed. If a myth, and, to a less degree, a tale, depend on a

nation's language—its modes of thought and expression—if the roots of the proper names be embedded in the language, and consequently obscured,
that myth and that tale must belong to that nation.
They belong to that nation's inheritance as much as
its language. Of course, care must be exercised in
deciding what is really the peculiar property of a
nation, and distinction made between the various
classes into which the materials of mythology and
folk-lore fall. " That certain deities occur in India,
Greece, and Germany, having the same names and
the same character, is a fact that can no longer be
denied.   That certain heroes, too, known to Indians,
Greeks, and Romans, point to one and the same
origin for these nations, both by their name and by
their history, is a fact by this time admitted by all
whose admission is of real value. As heroes are in
most cases gods in disguise, there is nothing startling
in the fact that nations who had worshipped the
same gods should also have preserved some common
legends of demigods or heroes, nay, even in a later
phase of thought, of fairies and ghosts. The case,
however, becomes much more problematical when
we ask whether stories also, fables told with a
decided moral purpose, formed part of that earliest
Aryan inheritance ? " Here Max Müller draws
a distinct line between fables with a moral or edu-
cative purpose and the rest of the materials of mythology, and he has clearly demonstrated that many
such are borrowed. The fables of Æsop have been

adopted into every language in Europe, and the moral tales of the Indians, after many vicissitudes, found a " local habitation " in the pages of La Fontaine and others. Another explanation for the distribution of myths is that primitive men worked in similar grooves wherever they lived ; man's circumstances being the same, his ideas and the expression of them will present strong resemblances everywhere. This view will account for the myths that are most widely distributed over the earth's surface. Jack the Giant-Killer, for instance, appears in the Zulu story of Uhlakanyana, who cheats the cannibal giant and his mother, to the latter of whom he had been delivered to be boiled, and whom he cunningly succeeds in substituting for himself. But the theory can apply only in a general way ; to the great body of myths common to certain nations it cannot apply at all ; it does not touch their deep and often detailed resemblances. What harmonises best with the facts of mythologic distribution is the grouping of nations into families proved to be genealogically allied from possessing a common body of myths and tales that must be descended from a parent stock. Although the facts of comparative mythology are sufficiently strong of themselves to prove the common origin of the nations from India to Ireland, yet it is satisfactory that the science of language has already proved the common descent of these nations, as far at least as language is concerned. Linguists have called the parent nation, from which they have sprung, the Aryan nation, a name which shall be adopted in this discussion. The only other group of nations that can satisfactorily be shown by their language and mythology to possess a common descent is the Semitic, which includes the Hebrews, Chaldeans, and Arabians. The Aryan and Semitic races have nothing in common, except what is borrowed, either in the matter of language or myth. When we are told that the Celtic god Bel is the same as the Semitic Baal, we may conclude that the assertion is, more than likely, both unscientific and untrue.

THE ARYAN NATION.

From the comparison of roots in the various present and past descendants of the original Aryan tongue, and, in a less degree, from a comparison of their myths, we are enabled to form a fair idea of the culture and religion of the Aryans. Not only can radical elements expressing such objects and relations as father, mother, brother, daughter, husband, brother-in-law, cow, dog, horse, cattle, ox, corn, mill, earth, sky, water, star, and hundreds more, be found identically the same, in the various branches of the Aryan tongue, now or sometime spoken, but they can also be proved to possess the elements of a mythological phraseology clearly descended from a common source. In the matter of culture, the

Aryans were organised in communities framed on the model of the patriarchal household. They had adopted a system of regular marriage with an elaborate grading of kinships and marriage affinities. In the household the father was king and priest, for there was also a family religion ; the wife and the rest of the family, though subservient to the *patria potestas*, were far from being slaves ; while, outside the household, grades and ranks of nobility or kinship were strictly marked. Comfortable houses and clustered villages, clearings and stations, with paths and roads were in existence ; the precious metals, together with copper, tin, and bronze, were in use, but iron was probably unknown. The domestic animals had long been tamed and named, for cattle and flocks composed their chief wealth, though the plough tilled the field and corn was grown and crushed in the mills and querns. They could count to one hundred at the very least, for the root of *ceud*, " *hund*-red," is common to all the descendant tongues, and they had divided the year into seasons and months—a fact which is especially proved by the root for *month* being taken from the name given to the moon, " the measurer." They spoke a language that was highly inflected and complex ; that is to say, the relation between words and the relations of time (or tense) and mood were expressed by changes in the terminations of words. On the whole, the Aryans were high in the barbaric state of culture, as opposed, on the one hand to the savage, and, on the other, to the civilised state of progress.

In regard to religion and Mythology, the Aryans were in much the same stage of advancement as in their culture generally. As their culture and language had required long ages to reach up to the state of comparative excellence at which they had arrived, so, too, their religion must have passed through lower phases until it reached the well developed cosmos of Aryan times. And as there are not wanting many signs of those earlier stages of belief both in Aryan Mythology and in the Mythologies of the descendant nations, it is necessary to glance briefly at what these stages may have been. Belief in the supernatural exists, and has existed, in all races of men whose beliefs we have any knowledge of. The lowest phase of this belief is known as " Animism," and consists in believing that what is presented to us in our dreams and visions has a real existence. Savage man makes no distinction between his dreaming and waking existence. He sees the " shadows " of the dead in his sleep, and firmly believes in their objective reality. But not merely the dead alone have shadows or spirits ; the living, too, have spirits or duplicates of self. Animals, also, and material objects, have souls, for is not the dead hero seen in dreams wearing the ghosts of arms —sword and hatchet, and such like—that he possessed in life ? The worship of ancestors would appear to have been the first form in which these beliefs took the shape of an active religion or worship of higher beings. Ancestor worship, though first, is by no means lost in subsequent stages, for of all forms it is the most persistent in its survival. Modern China and ancient Rome are prominent proofs of this fact. From ancestors, it is an easy step to worship the ghosts of other persons ; sometimes these were looked on as beneficent, and at other times as maleficent, beings, whose help was to be invoked or whose wrath was to be deprecated. Ghosts, ancestral and other, might inhabit natural objects—trees, rivers, wells, and animals ; and this, combined with the worship of the actual ghosts of these objects, sometimes gave rise to " fetishism," so well called the worship of " stocks and stones." Totemism, again, consists in the worship of a tribal badge ; some clan or nation worship a particular object, generally an animal, a form of worship which may easily have sprung from ancestor worship, since the ancestral ghost may have taken that particular form. Some go so far as to assert that the names of some of the Highland and Irish clans and their badges are remnants or remembrances of this worship, and appeal in proof is especially made to the clan " Chattan," with its animal crest, the cat. The next stage is the worship of the nature-spirits, or the natural powers as seen in objects of outward nature—clouds, lightning, and sky. This gives rise to polytheism proper, and, perhaps, prior to that, to henotheism, as Max Müller has so well named that "totemic" worship of one especial element of nature, making it for the moment the supreme deity with all the attributes that are applicable to it embellished and exhausted. In polytheism the plurality of deities is expressed ; in henotheism it is implied. Polytheism generally presents a dynastic system of gods under the rule of one supreme king or father, while henotheism implies a co-ordination of deities. "These deities," says Mr. Sayce, "are necessarily suggested by nature ; the variety of nature overpowers in an infantile state of society the unity for which the mind of man is ever yearning. Gradually, however, the attributes applied to the objects and powers of nature take the place of the latter ; the sun becomes Apollo, the storm Ares. Deities are multiplied with the multiplication of the epithets which the mythopoeic age changes into divinities and demi-gods, and side by side with a developed Mythology goes a developed pantheon. The polytheism, which the infinite variety of nature made inevitable, continues long after the nature worship that underlay it has grown faint and forgotten. A time at last comes when even abstract names have to submit to the common process ; temples are raised to Terror and Fear, to Love and Reverence ; and the doom of the old polytheism of nature is at hand. When once the spirit of divinity has been breathed into abstractions of the human mind, it cannot be long before their essential unity is recognised, and they are all summed up under the one higher abstraction of mono-theism."

But this quotation anticipates the history of Aryan Mythology in the descendant nations. Aryan religion itself was a fully developed henotheism, or rather a polytheism, where the Supreme Deity was different at different times in the eyes of the same worshipper. At one time, to take the Vedic hymns as representative of the oldest and nearest stratum of religious thought to the Aryan religion, Indra is the only god whom the singer recognises, and he exhausts his religious vocabulary on his praise alone ; and at another time Varuna receives all worship, at another it is Agni. Indra represents the heaven-god, more especially in the view of a rain-giving deity, for the root is the same as the English *water*, and is seen also in the sacred River Indus. Agni is the god of fire ; Varuna, of the canopy of heaven—the Greek Uranus. Comparing and analysing the ele-ments of Teutonic, Greek, and Hindu Mythology, for example, we may arrive at a tolerably clear conception of the Aryan pantheon and religious cultus. It would seem the chief deity was con-nected with the worship of light ; the shining canopy of heaven was the head of the Aryan Olympus. The Gaelic word *dia* (and *diu* day) ; Sanscrit, *Dyaus ;* Greek, *Zeus ;* Latin, *deus* and *Ju*-piter ; and English, *Tiw* (as seen in *Tues*day), are from the primitive name of this god, their common root being *div*, shining. Hence *dia* originally meant the bright sky, and Jupiter, the " sky-father," is the Roman version of " Father in Heaven." Fire, in all its manifestations, was an especial object of worship ; Agni is the Vedic name of this deity, which appears in Latin *ignis*, and Gaelic *ain* (heat). The sun and moon were prominent among the deities, the sun being the most in favour, perhaps, of all the gods. The epithets applied to him are innumerable, and, as a consequence, scarcely two nations have the same name for the sun-god, and nearly all have one or two deities that are phases of solar worship. The Sanscrit, *surya ;* Latin, *sol ;* English, *sun ;* and Gaelic, *solus*, present the chief root, the first four actually meaning the " sun," and being used as the name of the sun-deity often.

And there were other gods hardly inferior to these gods ; such were what we may call the " meteorological " deities—the regulators of weather and seasons. Prominent among these was the thunder god, who brings thunder and rain ; in the Vedic hymns his place is filled by the chief god Indra ; in Latin he is the Jupiter Tonans ; in the Norse Mythology, he appears as Thor who is next in importance to Odin himself ; and in the Celtic Mythology, he is known as Taranis. The storm god was worshipped under the title of Maruts, the Latin Mars, and Greek Ares. The wind had a high position among the deities, but among the descendant nations its position is not quite so high, unless we connect with it the god Hermes, who in Greek Mythology is clearly a wind god both in his connection with music and as messenger to the gods.

The gods we have hitherto discussed belong to the *intangible* objects of nature—the sky, stars, sun, dawn, and, perhaps, so too the " weather " gods. Max Müller gives two other possible classes of deified objects ; *semi-tangible* objects such as trees, mountains, the sea, the earth. These objects supply the material for what he calls the semi-deities. And thirdly, lowest of all, are *tangible* objects, such as " stocks and stones " and other elements of fetishism. The worship of semi-tangible objects shows clearly a remnant of the old animism, for these objects are endowed in savage culture with spirits of a personal type. " The lowest races," says Mr. Tylor, " not only talk of such nature-spirits, but deal with them in a thoroughly personal way, which shows how they are modelled on human souls. Modern travellers have seen North Americans paddling their canoes past a dangerous place on the river, and throwing in a bit of tobacco with a prayer to the river-spirit to let them pass. An African wood cutter who has made the first cut at a great tree has been known to take the precaution of pouring some palm-oil on the ground, that the angry tree-spirit coming out may stop to lick it up, while the man runs for his life. The state of mind to which these nature-spirits belong must have been almost as clearly remembered by the Greeks, when they could still fancy the nymphs of the lovely groves

and springs and grassy meadows coming up to the
council of the Olympian gods, or the dryads growing
with the leafy pines and oaks, and uttering screams
of pain when the woodman's axe strikes the trunk."
These nature spirits play a most important part
in folk-lore, appearing in the tales of the river demon,
the water kelpie, who drowns his victim in the whirl-
pool ; and in the giants, trolls, and dwarfs, who
represent mountain and earth spirits ; the healing
waters of sacred wells have only adopted saints'
names in place of the old pagan deities ; while the
little elves and fairies of the woods are but dim
recollections of the old forest spirits.

Of magic, a word or two may be said. It must be
remembered that the gods could change their shape
at pleasure ; their normal shape among Aryan
nations was the human, but they could assume the
shape of particular men or beasts, or even of inanimate objects, for Jupiter came into Danae's
prison in a shower of gold. Perseus' magical hat of
darkness and shoes of swiftness belong to the same
cloud-changing character. Spells and enchantments
form an important feature of magical powers, and
have their origin in spirit-explanations of the
numbing power of frost, the relaxing power of heat,
the power of drugs, as of the Indian Soma, and doubtless in the magnetic influence exerted by some men
and animals, notably the serpent. And if we descend
still lower, we find magic as a rule depend on a false
use of analogies. The Zulu who has to buy cattle

may be seen chewing a bit of wood, in order to soften the breast of the seller he is dealing with, for as the wood gets softer in his mouth, the sellers' heart is supposed also to soften. Such superstitions exist even in our own country to the present day. The writer of this has known of a case where a clay body, " corpan creadha," was actually made and stuck over with nails and pins, and placed in a stream channel to waste away. As the clay wasted, so with sharp pangs would waste away the person for whom it was intended.

The ethical side of the Aryan religion presented some interesting features. The contest between the powers of light and darkness—Dyaus and Indra on one side against Ahriman or Vritra, the bright sun-god against the snake-god of darkness, Apollo strangling the Python, represents a real ethical idea— good overcoming evil. Sacrifice and prayer, temple and altar, were known ; and sin and sin-offering were familiar ideas to the Aryans. A shadowy spirit existence after death was believed in ; heroes were taken to the halls of the gods, but the kingdom of Hades was the general abode of spirits, where the good and the evil got their deserts.

ARYAN MYTHS.

We shall now see how the Aryans dealt in one or two cases with the actions of their gods, and how this gave rise to a mythical life history of them in later times. It was around the sun-god that most of these myths were gathering. Offspring of night, whom he slays, he loves the dawn maiden, Daphne— " rosy-fingered morn," who flies from his embrace over the azure plains of Heaven, but, Cinderella-like, leaves a golden streak of light behind her whereby she may be followed and found. The sun has his toils too, in the pursuit ; storm-clouds intercept his path ; at times even the eclipse monster swallows him ; and he has to toil for mean creatures like men to give them light and heat, owing to the spells put upon him. But at length he overtakes, in the evening, his morning love, the dawn, now the evening dawn, who consoles him as he descends beneath the wave. In some such strains must the old Aryans have spoken of the sun's career and actions, and sung the praises of the Being who guided his flying coursers over the plains of Heaven. Later ages rationalised the myth into the loves and actions of Apollo and Daphne, Hercules and Dejanira, and others innumerable. The myth is broken down to a folk-tale, which appears in a variety of modern forms, of which the fairy tale of Cinderella is the best example. Cinderella is the youngest, as usual, of three sisters—the night-watches ; she is in fact the dawn maiden ; she is pursued by the young prince, and leaves her glass slipper—her streak of light—behind her, by means of which she is identified at last. This tale appears also in the

Gaelic popular stories. A king's daughter has to
fly with her fairy treasures—the peculiar thing is
that these maidens have always treasures, and there
generally is as much dispute about them as about the
maidens themselves ; these treasures appear to be
connected with the rain clouds, the cows and cattle
of the sun. The king's daughter takes service in
the new land she arrives in ; goes to a ball, unknown
to her employers, in her fairy dress ; creates a sen-
sation, so to speak ; but having to leave in haste,
she loses her glass slipper, whereby the enamoured
prince is enabled to find her. The tale of the
" Hoodie Crow," with which our discussion commenced, would appear to be a broken down myth
of the solar class ; and it is accordingly connected
with the nocturnal life of the sun-god, who then is
under the spell of the dark powers. The dawn
maiden pursues him through toils and difficulties,
and at last frees him from the spells.

Another fruitful source of myth and worship is
the change of summer into winter, when the earth
has to pass from the genial rule of the " fire " powers
to that of the " frost " king. The earth is spell-
bound during winter, by the machinations of the
frost-king ; the lovely goddess of summer has been
carried away, leaving her mother Earth discon-
solate ; " Proserpina gathering flowers, herself a
fairer flower, by gloomy Dis is gathered." She
becomes the wife of Pluto, god of the lower world,
but is allowed to return to her mother for half of the

year. Connected with this myth is the widespread tale of the imprisoned maiden. There are always three characters in the myth ; the monster or giant, who performs the abduction ; the maiden who is rich in treasures as well as beautiful ; and the youthful hero, the young Apollo, who is destined to overcome the monster and his spells.

Some minor points may briefly be noticed. Among the many names of the sun in the Veda, he is called the " golden-handed," a very natural simile for the golden rays shooting finger-like from him. The Hindus accordingly rationalise this, and tell how Savitri cut off his hand in a strait, and that the priests made a golden hand for him. The Norse god Tys (Zeus) had also his hand bitten off by the Fenris-wolf, and the Irish king of the De Dannans, Nuada of the Silver Hand, lost his hand in fight with the Firbolg giant, and the physician Diancet made him a silver one. Another wide-spread myth is to be referred to the same source ; the sun-god Apollo is the best of archers—the " Far-darter," of Homeric poetry. In nearly every Aryan nation there is a historical legend telling the doughty deed of some great archer ; such is the story of Tell, in Switzerland, which is typical of the rest. The legend appears in the German tale of Eigel, brother of Wayland, the smith-god ; while in Braemar it is circumstantially told regarding the ancestor of the Machardies, also a " smith " family. Of myths arising from the wind, storm, thunder, earth, and

sea, it is unnecessary to speak as yet ; they will
appear in their proper place among the folk-tales,
and some—as the sea-deities, Lir and his children—
among the myths of the heroes.

RESULTS OF THE GENERAL PRINCIPLES.

The peculiar characteristics of Mythology have now
been indicated ; the cause of myth, and the wide
diffusion of the same myths among different nations
have been discovered respectively in the philosophy
of primitive man, and the common descent of the
chief European and Asiatic nations. It has been
shown that the Aryan nation possessed what may
be dignified with the name of a civilisation ; its
culture and religion were of a very high type, though
there were not wanting numerous traces of the
culture of more primitive and ruder times. It
now becomes our duty to follow the fortunes of the
Mythology of one of the nations descended from
this Aryan parent nation, and see how it shaped
the common heritage.

It may be set down as a general principle that the
Celts ought not to have in their language, mythology, or customs, any features inconsistent with
their Aryan descent ; they may have developed the
outward and inward features of Aryan civilisation,
according to the idiosyncracies of the Celtic race,
but the essential Aryan characteristics ought still

to be recognisable in the descendant Celtic languages and myths. Whatever we find in these must conform, regard being had to the development of Celtic peculiarities, to what we know to have been true of the myths and language of the parent Aryan tongue, or of those of one or two of the other Aryan nations. Anything in Celtic myth, language, or customs, inconsistent with an Aryan descent, or of a plainly non-Aryan character, must first of all be distrusted until its existence among the Celts, and them alone, has been established on indubitable grounds. Nor must explanations of Celtic phenomena be accepted which would imply relationship with races outside the Aryan stock—such as with the Semitic or Hebrew race, until clear historical or other proof is adduced. The *a priori* argument against such a connection is so strong that special care must be exercised in allowing non-Aryan explanations to appear. It is needless to remark that until lately the Celts suffered much from the injudicious and unscientific theories of Celtic enthusiasts, and it has been only by the patient industry of the Germans that full recognition has been given to the proper position of the Celts among the other Indo-European nations. Even yet, in Scotland, too little attention is paid to the scientific facts established in Celtic ethnology and philology. For this state of matters there is now little excuse, more especially as within the last year or two the results of Continental and British learning have been put before the public in the works of Mr.

Elton and Professor Rhys, to both of whom the present writer must express his great obligations.

SOURCES OF INFORMATION.

Of the old Celtic nations—their culture and their rel gion—we have no native account. No Celtic language has got any literary remains earlier than the seventh century at farthest, and even these are but glosses or marginal Gaelic equivalents of Latin words in manuscripts. The oldest manuscripts of connected works cannot be traced farther back than the eleventh century. By this period Christianity had asserted its sway, at least in name, and the old paganism remained only in the customs and the heroic and folk-tales of the nation. What religion existed in Ireland and Britain a thousand years before this period of the oldest manuscripts must be discovered, if it can at all, from some other source than contemporary native evidence. Yet we are not without a fair idea of what the old Celtic religion was. The sources of our information in deciphering what Professor Rhys has called " the weather worn history " of the Celts are these : Roman and Greek writers have left contemporary accounts of Celtic history, religion, and customs, though in the case of religion and customs, such accounts are scrappy indeed, and the history is generally a statement

of contemporary actions and the relations of the
Celts to the favoured races of Rome and Greece.
Next to these come the monuments and inscriptions
of ancient Gaul and Britain. These comprise mostly
the votive inscriptions to the deities, the statues,
and the coinage of the period. The names of places,
especially of rivers, have indicated Celtic localities,
migrations, and religious beliefs ; for how numerous
are, for instance, the rivers with the name Dee
(goddess), showing the wide-spread worship of water
and rivers among the Celts ? Examination also of
the rude stone monuments and the barrows of pre-
historic times has elucidated much that is dark
in Celtic History, while the examination of physical
characteristics in the race has helped even more to
clear up difficulties of ethnology. A judicious use
of the oldest heroic and folk tales must divulge
some secrets in regard to Mythology, if not to history ;
while modern folk-tales and customs lend special
aid in reflecting light on the past. An intelligent
scrutiny of the Roman calendar of saints will disclose
a few more Celtic divinities in the realms of saint-
dom ; for where the Church did not make demons
or heroes of the ancient gods, it did the next best
thing—it made saints of them.   In the same way we
can recognise Pagan festivals and customs in a
Christian guise ; the Church festivals are nearly
all the result of assimilating the existing religious
customs.   And, lastly, to steady our whole results,
we have to remember that the Celts are an Aryan

people, and that explanations of their customs and religions must follow the ordinary lines of the other Aryan nations. Where there are differences—and there are many such—these must be caused by the fact that the Celts assimilated with themselves an earlier population. Notice has already been taken of the Pictish law of succession, where descent is traced through the mother. This implies clearly a low view of the state of matrimony, and one clearly opposed to an Aryan source. We are therefore fairly justified in regarding the Picts as strongly admixed with a non-Aryan race.

In thus reconstruct'ng the past history of the Celts, at least three classes of *savants* are pressed into our service. First and foremost is the philologist, who has within the last generation or two completely revolutionised the science of ethnology. He has shown in the clearest manner possible the common descent of most of the European nations, at least as far as language is concerned, and that means a vast amount, for language is followed by a common mythology, and, in a less degree, by common customs. The next savant we draw upon is the anthropologist, or, rather, the physiologist ; he examines the remains of ancient man and the characteristics of modern man, and classifies accordingly. And, thirdly, we have the archæologist, who examines prehistoric remains and implements. These three classes of workers do not well agree ; Professor Huxley despises the ethnological results of linguistic science, while Professor Rhys does not conceal his contempt for those who decide on national descent by " skin and skull ; " and Mr. Fergusson will not leave his " rude stone monuments " to consider what either of them may say. Two such men as Mr. Tylor and Mr. Elton are, therefore, to the ordinary student, simply invaluable guides, from the fact that they attempt to combine the researches of all three. From the materials collected from these three sources, we shall proceed to give a short account of the Celts and their religion.

THE CELTS.

When or where the people lived who spoke the original Aryan tongue is not known with any certainty. " It seems probable," says one writer, " that their home was somewhere in South-western Asia, and the time of their dispersion not less than three thousand years before Christ." Fick holds that they split up first into two parts, answering to the modern Asiatic and European Aryans. The European branch again broke up into two—the South-western European division and the Northern European division. The latter included the Slavonic (Russians and old Prussians), and the Teutonic (English, Germans, Norse, &c.,) races ; while the Southern branch comprised the Greek, Latin, and Celtic races. The order in which they are enumer-

ated above shows the order of their arrival in Europe ;
first came the Celts leading the van of the Southern
division, while the Sclavs brought up the rear of all.
It has been remarked that for the purpose of attaining
political greatness the Celts came too soon, the Sclavs
too late. The line of Celtic migration across Europe
has been traced in the names of places, especially
the river names. The Don and the Dnieper would
appear to prove that they crossed the Russian
steppes. Yet there are evident traces of the Celts
on the Ægean sea, and we have the River Strumon
on the Thracian coast, which is clearly Celtic from the
existence of the *s*, which was lost in Greek itself ;
and we may add the famous Mount Pindus in
Greece.* In any case, however, be their route
whatever we please, we find the Celts in the earliest
records we have of them in possession of the greatest
portion of Western Europe. At the time of their
taking Rome in 390 B.C., the Celts would appear
to have possessed, as they certainly did two centuries
later, Nothern Italy, France, Belgium, and part of
Germany, most of Spain, Britain, and Ireland.
How much of the middle of Europe they then held
is unknown, but that they did possess part of what
now is Germany is clear from the names of places,
and also from the fact that the Germans have, in
common with the Celts, many myths which must
have then been absorbed by the Germans in absorbing
the Celtic population. About 220 B.C. the Romans

---

* See Kuhn's Beitraege, Vol. viii., p. 4.

conquered Nothern Italy, a hundred years later they
conquered the Mediterranean coast of France, and
seventy years afterwards Cæsar conquered the whole
of France and completely crushed the Gallic power.

That is briefly the political side of their history.
But there are two points to notice in their internal
history of special importance in the present inquiry.
The Celts, in entering Europe, found the country
inhabited, and this previous population, a non-
Aryan one of course, they either exterminated or
absorbed. It is, therefore, of vital importance
to know as much as possible about this previous
population, for, naturally, its customs, beliefs, and,
in a much less degree, its language, were absorbed
by the conquering Celt. From the evidence of
language and customs alone, Professor Rhys has,
in his work on " Celtic Britain," been able to prove
the existence of a previous non-Celtic and non-
Aryan population in Britain. The Pictish custom
of succession already mentioned, and the continual
reference in classical writers to some British nations
who had community of wives—Cæsar erroneously
attributes this to all Britain alike, Celt and non-Celt
—point to a low idea of matrimony that must have
belonged to the previous population. Again, in
the list of Kings given for the Picts, the names are
not of an Aryan or Celtic type ; Aryan names were
always compounds, however much denuded by time,
but these Pictish names are monosyllabic and un-
meaning. The frequency of animal names in Pictish

districts has also been adduced as a proof in the same direction, though not a convincing argument, for most nations have animal names among their personal names. Mr. Elton has pointed out some peculiar legal customs with regard to the right of the youngest son to succeed to the father's property, and these, he thinks, indicate a non-Aryan source. But the matter is rendered practically a certainty, if we summon to our aid the physiologist. He finds the British nation divided into two or more races. These are, at the least, the small dark-skinned race and the fair-skinned race. " All the Celts," says Mr. Elton, " according to a remarkable consensus of authorities, were tall, pale, and light-haired." The dark-skinned race evidently belong to a different race from the Celts, and when we consider that Europe has been inhabited for several thousand years, and that men have existed here who used stone weapons, and thereafter bronze, before iron came into vogue, which it probably did along with the Celts, we must believe that there was a race before the Celts in Europe, who used stone and bronze weapons. But the evidence does not stop here. From the contents of the barrows and tombs of the stone and bronze ages, it has been proved by the skeletons and skulls that there were two races at least previous to the Celts ; one race being the dark-skinned and small one already mentioned, with long skulls ; the other with fair skin and hair and broad skulls, a tall race, rough-featured, beetle-browed, with the nose overhung at its root, heavy cheek-bones, and prominent chin ; these last differing much from the straight-faced, oval-headed men who are recognised as Celts and Aryans. The dark-skinned race of Britain is called the " Silurian," from the ancient tribe so named by Tacitus in the Vale of the Severn, and described by him as " Iberian" in appearance. The fair race Mr. Elton designates the " Finnish," from its apparent Finnish or Ugrian affinities. The Picts would appear to be for the most part of this race, doubtless, with a strong admixture in after times of the pure Celtic stock. The archæologist, unfortunately, cannot help us much, but it is believed that this Finnish race were the builders of the huge stone monuments scattered all over Europe—dolmens, cromlechs, and Druid circles, while the barrows of both the ante-Celtic races exist.

The influence exerted by these previous races on Celtic customs and religion must doubtless have been considerable. " The strangeness of the ' lower mythology ' prevailing in Wales and Britanny might afford some evidence in favour of its pre-Celtic origin. But no country in Europe is free from those gross superstitions which seem to indicate an underworld of barbarism and remnants of for-gotten nations not wholly permeated by the culture of the dominant races." Professor Rhys goes so far as to refer Druidism to the Silurian race, because Cæsar mentions Britain as the birthplace of that cultus, and it is of a character which he considers non-Aryan. It is almost certain that second-sight and other ecstatic moods must be referred to the pre-Celtic races.

WELSH AND GAELS.

The second point in the internal history of the Celts is the fact that the race is divided into two great divisions, caused by the languages used by each. The difference between Welsh and Gaelic is very great, yet not so great as to preclude their being classed as one race, making up one of the Aryan branches. The difference between the two languages can be traced as far back as history goes, and, by monuments and inscriptions can be followed back for two thousand years, when still the Gaelic race was very different in language from the Welsh or British. It would appear that the Celts overran Europe in two successive waves of conquest. The first wave was the Gaelic one ; it was followed by the Welsh— we may rather call it the Gaulish wave. The Gauls pushed the Gaels from France into Britain and Ireland, and then followed them into Britain. When British history begins with the Christian era, France and Belgium were Gaulish or Welsh-speaking, and so also was the Eastern part of England, and the Scotch Lowlands ; while Cornwall and Devon, most of Wales, Cumberland, Galloway, and the surrounding counties, north of the Forth, and all Ireland

belonged to the Gaels. It must be remembered
that a good portion of the population north of the
Grampians were probably non-Celtic. By the end
of the seventh century of this era no Gael lived in
England ; the British tribes had been driven back
to the corners of the country by the Saxons, and they
absorbed the old Gaelic population. Ireland was
still altogether Celtic, and so remained practically
till the 13th century and later.

The last wave of the Celts was in its turn pressed
on from two sides. First the Romans overran
and garrisoned Gaul, and then England, which they
kept for four hundred years, much as we keep India
at present. Then the Teutonic nations pressed
on France from the north, conquered it and were
absorbed ; while in England they conquered and
absorbed the old population, leaving the old Welsh
population to the western shores. The eastern
portion of Ireland was conquered and settled in,
and the rest has been gradually falling under the
sway of the English tongue. The Celtic-speaking
peoples at present are the Bretons of Britanny,
the Welsh, the Irish, and the Highlanders. The
total number who can understand a Celtic tongue
is, according to M. Sebillot, three millions and a
half (*Rev. Celt.*, *iv.*, 278).

CELTIC CHARACTERISTICS.

Of the physical characteristics of the Celts, except
to show unity or diversity of descent, it would be

needless to speak in discussing their mythology ;
but there are so many Irish legends bearing upon
the early ethnology of these islands, with continual
reference to small dark men, tall brown-haired and
fair-haired races, that it is necessary to at least
glance at the question. The unanimity of ancient
opinion in making the Celts tall and fair-haired
has already been noticed, and in the myths the ideal
of beauty is, as a rule, what is told of the summer
isles of the West, where dwelt a divine race of the
pure Celtic type, " long-faced, yellow-haired hunters "
and goddesses with hair like gold or the flower of the
broom. Another type of beauty was recognised :
Peredur or Percival of Wales, as well as the lady
Deirdre of Irish story, would have no consort unless
the hair was black as the raven's wing, the skin as
white as snow, and the two red spots in the cheeks
as red as the blood of the bird which the raven was
eating in the snow. But, " if you look at the Celtic
countries," says the author of " Loch-Etive and the
Sons of Uisnach," " that is, countries in which
Celtic was spoken in old time, or is spoken now, you
find a predominance of dark hair." There would
seem, therefore, to have been a decided change in
the colour of the hair among the Celts since the
times of Cæsar and Tacitus ; but whether this is due
to mingling of races or is connected with a higher
nervous activity, for fair-haired children become
dark-haired as the nervous system becomes more
active by years, is a question which, though im-

portant for the mythologist to know in its bearing
on the migration and borrowing of myths and
manners, yet cannot be decided in the present state
of knowledge.   We have still among us the remnants
of the small dark people, and, if Professor Rhys
is right, the Highlands must mostly in race be of
the fair Finnish type that anteceded the Celts, with
just sufficient of the Celtic conqueror among them
as to take his language and general manners.

There, is, however, a more wonderful agreement
in the mental characteristics formerly attributed
to the Celts with what we now regard as the Celtic
character.   Roman writers have noticed their won-
wonderful quickness of apprehension, their im-
pressibility and great craving for knowledge, qualities
which have rendered the Celt a very assimilable
being in the fusion of races.   They were generous
to a degree ; prompt in action, but not very capable
of sustained effort.   Cæsar is never tired speaking
of the " mobilitas "—changeableness—of the Gauls,
and also of their " celerity," both mental and physical.
Another feature noticed from the very first, and still
noticeable in the Celts, is their fondness for colour ;
" loudness," we might say, both in colour and sound,
musical or other, has been especially attractive to
them.   They appear in flaming tartan dresses before
the walls of Rome in 390 B.C., as we see from both
Livy and Virgil.   " They wear," says Diodorus
Siculus, a writer of the 1st century, B.C., " bracelets
and armlets, and round their necks thick rings, all

of gold, and costly finger rings, and even golden corselets ; they have dyed tunics, flowered with colours of every kind, and striped cloaks fastened with a brooch, and divided into numerous many-coloured squares." In this description we have the tartan, but unfortunately the kilt had not yet made its appearance ; the Gauls and ancient Britons actually wore tartan trousers ! Their love of ornament and colour appears strongly in the mythic tales equally of Wales, Ireland, and the Highlands ; indeed, so rich is the description in one Welsh tale that at the end of it we are told that " no one knows the ' Dream of Rhonabwy ' without a book, neither bard nor gifted seer ; because of the various colours that were on the horses, and the many wondrous colours of the arms, and of the panoply and of the precious scarfs, and of the virtue-bearing stones."

We can trace among the Celts the same succession of political life that we find in some of the other Aryan nations, notably the Greeks and the Romans. The patriarchal system of Aryan times had given place on European soil to kings, who were merely larger editions of the patriarch of old. They were kings of the Homeric type ; for the Irish kings are not accurately represented in the lives of the saints as Pharaohs surrounded with Druids and magicians. The king consulted the chiefs beneath him, and the people, after this consultation, were told of his pleasure, but could only, apparently, murmur approval or disapproval. In the course of time,

the chiefs abolished the kingly power, and conducted
matters themselves as an oligarchy, often cruelly
oppressing the common people. In Greece, the
oligarchy was overthrown by some clever man who
sided with the common people and, through them,
made himself " tyrant," as they called it. The
last step was the abolition of tyranny and the setting
up of a democracy. Rome shows much the same
historical sequence, only the tyrant does not appear ;
the oligarchy extended some privileges to the commons, and a sort of union was established, which,
however, in the end, failed, and gave place to an
Imperial sway. Among the Gauls we have distinct
traces of all these phenomena, " though," as Professor Rhys says, " no Gaulish Herodotus or Livy
was found to commit them to the pages of history."
Gaul would appear to have just passed through the
stage when tyrants and oligarchs were struggling
with the people ; for Cæsar found everywhere " the
sulking and plotting representatives of the fallen
dynasties, and readily turned them into use, either
in bringing information about what was going on
in the senates of the peoples who had expelled their
ancestors from the office of king, or in keeping their
states in subjection by appointing them kings in
the room of their fathers and under Roman protection." No wonder then that Cæsar tells us that
Gaul was torn asunder by factions. Britain had
yet retained its kings, and appears to have lost
them only when the Island was conquered by the

Romans. Ireland had its five kings even within historic times ; and the history of Scotland during the Stuart period shows how nearly an oligarchy came to rule this country.

The old Celtic population of both Gaul and Britain appears to have been very prosperous. They were excellent farmers, but their chief riches lay in their cattle ; and their food, especially in Britain, was mostly flesh, milk, and cheese. Posidonius, in the first century before Christ, has left us a description of a Gaulish banquet which is important as reflecting light on the myths and tales of later Irish times. He was delighted at the antique simplicity of his entertainers, and amused at their Gallic frivolity and readiness for fighting at meal times. " They were just like the people in Homer's time." The guest was not asked his name or the purpose of his journey until the feast was over. They sat on a carpet of rushes or on the skins of animals in front of little tables. There was plenty of meat, roast and boiled, which they ate, after the fashion of lions, gnawing the joint, but they would at times use their small bronze knives, kept in a separate sheath by the side of the sword. Beer was their drink, which they poured through their long moustaches like water through a sieve or funnel. " The minstrels sang and the harpers played, and, as the company drank, they bowed to the right in honour of their god. The guests sat in three rings—nobles, shield-bearers, and javelin-men—all in order of their pre-

cedence." If they quarrelled about the food, they
would get up and fight it to the death ; and sometimes the guests were entertained with swordplay,
and sometimes even a man would consent to die
to amuse the rest, so careless were they of life.   Their
conduct and appearance in battle and in the chase
are no less important for us to notice.   " We seem,"
says Mr. Elton, " to see the Brigantian soldier, with
his brightly-painted shield, his pair of javelins and
his sword hilt ' as white as the whale's-bone : '
his matted hair supplied the want of a helmet, and
a leather jerkin served as a cuirass.   When the line
of battle was formed, the champions ran out to
insult and provoke the foe ; the chiefs rode up and
down on their white chargers shining in golden
breastplates, others drove the war chariots along the
front, with soldiers leaning out before their captain
to cast their spears and handstones : the ground
shook with the prancing of horses, and the noise of
the chariot wheels.   We are recalled to scenes of
old Irish life which so strangely reproduce the world
of the Greek heroes and the war upon the plains of
Troy.   We see the hunters following the cry of the
hounds through the green plains and sloping glens ;
the ladies at the feast in the woods, the game roasting
on the hazel-spits, ' fish and flesh of boar and badger,'
and the great bronze cauldrons at the fireplace in
the cave.   The hero, Cuchulain, passes in his chariot
brandishing the heads of the slain ; he speaks with
his horses, the Gray and ' Dewy-Red,' like Achilles

on the banks of Scamander.   The horses, in Homeric
fashion, weep tears of blood and fight by their
master's side ; his sword shines redly in his hand,
the ' light of valour ' hovers round him, and a goddess
takes an earthly form to be near him and to help
him in the fray."

THE GAULISH RELIGION.

The religion of the Gauls is the only Celtic religion
of which we have any description, such as it is, left.
Now, we should be justified in assuming that the
Gaulish religion is fairly representative of what the
old religion of the British and Irish Celts was, even
though we had not Tacitus' direct testimony to this
being the case. The descriptions we have of the
Gaulish religion are sufficiently meagre. Three
chapters of Cæsar, a few lines from Diodorus, Mela,
and Strabo, some scattered allusions in Pliny,
fifteen lines from Lucan, and a statement from the
Greek Timagenes reproduced in Ammianus Marcellinus, are practically all our authorities. The
statues and inscriptions preserved to our time are
almost our only authority for the names of the deities;
while the calendar of the Church saints, local
festivities and traditions, render some little help
in this and also in matters of ritual.

Cæsar's sketch of the Gaulish pantheon, though
meagre, is yet the best. We owe it entirely to the
fact that for practical purposes the Gaulish religion

was much the same as the Roman, with the exception
of Druidism, which he doubtless saw would be a
source of danger, unless it could be assimilated to
Roman ideas and practices. We are, therefore,
prepared, from our knowledge of the Aryan descent
of the Celts, to believe what Cæsar says when he
writes that the ideas of the Gauls with regard to the
gods were much the same as those of other nations,
meaning especially Romans and Greeks. He tells
us that the god most worshipped was Mercury ;
that is to say, the Gaulish god was not named
Mercury, but corresponded in his attributes to that
Roman deity. Cæsar, unfortunately, does not
record the native names for these deities. They
regarded Mercury as the inventor of arts, presiding
over trade and commerce, and means of communi-
cation between people. After him came the deities
answering to the Roman Apollo, Mars, Jupiter,
and Minerva ; Apollo drove away diseases, Minerva
taught the useful arts of life, Jupiter held the sway
of Heaven, and Mars ruled the department of war.
To Mars they would vow what they should capture
in war, and when they conquered they would sacrifice
the cattle, and heap up the other wealth in mounds,
in consecrated places, and no one would dare touch
or steal these treasures, both from fear of the gods
and from the extreme cruelty of the punishment
that would follow detection. Cæsar also notices
a feature of Celtic character which is still persistent
in the race. The nation, he says, is very much

given to religious matters. And on this account, he proceeds, those who are affected with diseases of a rather serious character, and those who are in great dangers, either sacrifice human beings, or make a vow to that effect ; and at these sacrifices they employ the Druids. They think, he says, that the Deity cannot be appeased unless human life is given up for human life, and they have even national sacrifices of this kind. They make huge images of wickerwork, inside which they place human beings alive ; and this they set on fire, and the victims perish. Generally the victims are criminals, but if criminals are wanting, they have recourse to innocent persons. These human sacrifices seem horrible to our modern minds, and to the Romans, though familiar with the idea of human sacrifice, for in the time of the Second Punic war, they, themselves, resorted in their religious terror to the sacrificing of a male and female Gaul, and it was not until the 1st century before Christ that the Senate formally forbade such sacrifices even in Rome—to the Romans even the Gauls appeared reckless in their massacres, such occurring, too, when there did not appear to be any special danger. Strabo says that it was a tenet of the Druids that the harvest would be rich in proportion to the richness of the harvest of death.

Another article of the Gaulish creed is given by Cæsar. The Gauls, he says, assert that they are all sprung from Pluto (the god of the lower world), for so the Druids teach. Hence, therefore, they

reckon by nights instead of days.   In regard to
the belief which Cæsar records, it is probably only
a mythical way of recording a belief common to
most nations in their barbarous state, that they are
the aboriginal inhabitants and sprung from the
soil on which they dwell.   As to the Gauls reckoning
by nights instead of days, Cæsar is scarcely right in
tracing to it the belief that they are sprung from
Pluto ; the Greeks originally thus counted their time,
and the Germans also computed their time the same
way, just as we still speak of fortnights and " sen-
nights," while the Welsh word for week, *wythnos*,
means " eight-nights."   The mythical meaning of
the custom is quite clear ; the night was supposed
to give birth to the day and the sun ; for Chaos is
before Kosmos, Night before Day, in mythology.
Hence the night is before the day in the order of
time.   This fact is embodied in the well-known
Gaelic expression, " Thig an oidhche roimh 'n latha,"
which applies to all the festivals of the calendar,
with the exception of that referred to in the other
phrase, " An Inid bheadaidh, thig an latha roimh
'n oidhche."

We have thus seen from Cæsar that in the Gaulish
religion a Pluto reigned in darkness, and a Jupiter
in heaven ; that Mars was the lord of war ; that
Apollo, Mercury, and Minerva brought precious
gifts to mankind.   The poet Lucan has preserved
to us, though in an obscure fashion, the names of
three Gaulish gods in the celebrated lines—

" Et quibus immitis placatur sanguine diro
Teutates horrensque feris altaribus Esus,
Et Taranis Scythicae non mitior Dianae."

We have here the grim Teutates, Esus with fearful
sacrifices, and Taranis, whose altars were no less
cruel than those of Scythian Diana. Of Esus but
little can be said ; no trace of him exisits outside
Gaul, where statues and, at least, one inscription
bearing his name have been found. Teutates, likely
from the same root as the Gaelic *tuath*, people, has
been identified with various deities ; probably he
was the war-god, defender of the people, at whose
altars captives poured forth their blood. It does
no appear that his name was used on British soil ;
Mr. Elton thinks that his place in this country
was filled by " Camulus," a word which appears
on British coins in connection with warlike emblems,
and is used as a compound in the names of several
military stations of the Roman period. Taranis
was the Northern Jupiter, worshipped by the Britons,
also, under epithets derived from the words for
thunder and rain. He answers to the Norse god
Thor, the head of the " meteorological " gods, who
regulate the weather and the seasons—" who can
withhold the rain and the dew, or blacken the
heavens with clouds and wind, or drive in the tempest
with chariot and horses of fire." The Irish *Dinn-
Senchus* mentions this " thunder " god as " Etirun,
an idol of the Britons."

Two other names of deities are preserved to us in

the classical writers.   Lucian speaks of a sort of
Gaulish Hercules, represented as an old man drawing
a large multitude after him by cords fastened to their
ears and his tongue, and he was their god of letters
and eloquence, and they called him Ogmios.   This
name appears afterwards as that of the Irish sacred
or runic alphabet, so named from its inventor, Ogma,
the son of Elathan, evidently a degraded deity.
Again, one or two other writers mention the god
Belenus, a name common in inscriptions and in proper
names of persons.   The inscriptions also give, according to the Gallo-Romanic habit, the Latin God
as well, with whom he was identified : we have
such a combination often as Belenus Apollo, thus
making him the equivalent to the Roman sun and
healing-god.   This Belenus is the famous deity of
the Druids according to the school of Neo-Druidists,
the investigators into the system of the Druids,
lately rampant among us.   As a rule, Belenus, or
rather Bel, as he was called by them, was identified
with the Phenician Baal, and no end of theories
were started on such suppositions.   The word
Belenus may, however, be from the same root as
Apollo, and probably is from that root, as Mr.
Moberly has pointed out in his notes to Cæsar.   That
his worship was connected with solar rites is evident
from the manner in which Ausonius describes his
temple at Bayeux ; but he was also especially
connected with health-giving waters and herbs
and was worshipped at medicinal resorts under

various local titles, the most important of which
are Borvo (Bourbon) and Grannus. The latter
title is doubtless connected with the Gaelic *grian*,
sun, and it is interesting to note that an altar was
once found at Inveresk with the inscription, "Apollini
Granno," which clearly shows the worship of this
sun-god in ancient Scotland. It is probably in connection with the service of Belenus that the cutting
of the mistletoe took place, as related by Pliny.
The passage is given either in full or in abstract
in almost all our school books of history, and it is
there wrongly given out as a "Druidic" rite. It
is merely a case of herb worship, common to all
nations. The mistletoe is far more famous in
Teutonic Mythology, and the gallant rites at modern
Christmases are merely a remembrance of its ancient
efficacy as a preserver and defender from harm.
Pliny tells us that on the sixth day of the moon,
the commencement of the Gaulish month, a Druid
or priest, clothed in white, mounted the tree and cut
the plant with a golden sickle. It was received on
a white cloth, and two white bulls were sacrificed,
while the people burst forth in prayer for the favour
of the god. The mistletoe was supposed thus to be
a cure for sterility, and a safeguard against poisons.
This is just merely a form of *fetishism*.

The Gaulish inscriptions give us quite a host of
minor deities. The Roman system of assimilating
conquered peoples appears extremely well in these
inscriptions ; in nearly every case the Roman deity

is given as the principal name to which is attached
as epithet the local Gaulish equivalent. We, therefore, meet w th combinations like these : " Marti
Segomoni," " Marti Caturigi," " Mercurio Artaio,"
" Iovi Bagniati," " Apollini Virotuti," etc. The
Gaulish and British goddess, Belisama, is the most
important to notice ; she answered to the Latin
Minerva, goddess of arts, who, along with " Mercury,"
was the most human of all the deities of Gaul. The
goddesses of the healing springs were honoured as
the companions of Apollo. " Divine beings everywhere mediated between man and heaven." Fountains, rivers, and hills had their deities, and the sea-
nymph of the Breton shore is still revered under the
title of St. Anne. Every village was protected by
local deities, with the generic title of " Matris " or
" Mothers," names which appear in great numbers
on the inscriptions, and which survive, we are told,
in mediæval legends as the White Ladies, the " Three
Fairies," the Weird Sisters, and the Wild Women
of the Woods. Some, again, of the lesser deities
appear as the giants of our folk-tales. Such has
been the fate of " Gargantua," an old Gaulish deity
of Normandy, whose festivals are not unknown yet,
and whose fame appears on the pages of Rabelais.
There were also innumerable private or family
gods, answering to the Roman Penates and Lares,
of whom inscriptions and statues testify.

DRUIDISM.

One feature of the Gaulish religion still remains to be discussed, and that, too, perhaps its most important one. We have discussed the religious beliefs of the people, but not their ecclesiastical polity. This is known as Druidism, although that term is commonly made to include all that we know of the Gaulish religion as well. But the Druids were rather the philosophers and divines of the Gauls ; and, as what we know of their opinions and practices is somewhat remarkable, it is better not to confuse their system with the ordinary Aryan religion of the Gauls. Here, again, it must be repeated that our information is meagre ; in fact, with regard to the Druids no less meagre, and far more unsatisfactory than our comparatively poor information about their general religion. Indeed, with the addition of two chapters in Cæsar, a sentence in Cicero, and nigh a dozen lines of Lucan, our authorities for Druidism are included in the enumeration already made in regard to Gaulish religion in general. No monuments or inscriptions can help us, nor can we trust in the slightest degree the references made to Druidism by early Irish or Welsh writers : the Druids of Irish history are mere conjurors and magicians. Neither can any customs or religious survivals be referred to Druidic belief or usage. But it may be at the start premised that there is, perhaps, little to know, and that it is entirely due to Cæsar's account of them, probably itself somewhat exaggerated in its political aspect, and certainly misread by modern writers under the influence of their knowledge of mediæval ecclesiasticism, that this exaggerated opinion of Druidism is prevalent. So little is known, and the little that is known is so interesting, that it opened quite a new world for fancies and speculations. " Omne ignotum pro magnifico est ; " the unknown passes for the magnificent. Here was an unknown and unknowable land, where in circular temples of stone, and mid groves of oak, in vestments of stainless white, and ornaments of glittering gold, stalked majestically the Druids, holding high converse with their disciples on the nature of the one God—for such philosophers could only be monotheists !—on the immortality of the soul, the courses of the stars, and, in fact, on all the mighty problems of life. Dr. Smith tells us that they alone kept the first tradition of monotheism intact in the West ; and Reynaud, but a generation ago, found in their human sacrifices only the consequence of the idea, dominant now as in the days of the Druids, that the higher the victim the more complete the atonement offered to the Deity for the sins of man. John Toland, at the end of the 17th century, an Irishman of fertile imagination and advanced opinions, possessed of no small learning, was the first to lead the way into the undiscovered country of Druidism.

The references in Pliny were made to disclose a pomp and ritual that could vie with the best days of the Church of Rome ; surplices of white—incidentally worn, as may be seen from Pliny—were their usual dress, with golden ornaments, sacrifice utensils and amulets, all of gold. The megalithic monuments— circles, cromlechs, and menhirs, were of course their work—their temples and their altars, and these also showed their knowledge of the mechanical powers. Nay, cairns and barrows were Druidic remains, and vetrified forts ! Everything unexplained in archæological monuments, in social customs, and in proverbial language must be Druidic. Dr. Smith, of the " Seann Dana," followed Toland and made a most unscrupulous use of his classical authorities. Welsh and French writers took the same view of the old religion of Gaul, and Celtomania reigned supreme in this obscure region, until lately the light of modern criticism was allowed to shine through the overhanging mist of nonsensical speculation.

All that can with certainty be known of the Druids will first be briefly given, apart from any personal theories. Cæsar is again our first and best authority. In the digression in his 6th book, on the manners and customs of the Gauls and Germans, he tells us that all men of any consideration or position were included among either the Druids or the nobles. The Druids conduct public and private sacrifices, and interpret omens. Young men flock to them for

instruction ; and they are held in great honour ;
for they have the decision of all controversies, public
and private ; they are judges in cases of crime,
murder, and disputes in regard to succession or
boundaries ; and whoever abides not by their decision is excommunicated—a most severe punishment, for such are reckoned sacrilegists, and men
flee from their presence for fear of disaster from
contact with them. A chief Druid presides over
them, having supreme authority. He may be
elected with or without voting, and they at times
resort to war to decide the matter. They meet
at an appointed time of the year in the territories
of the Carnutes, in the middle of Gaul, where there
is a consecrated place ; and there all come who
have disputes, and abide by their decisions. It is
thought that the system was founded in Britain, and
thence transferred to Gaul, and those who at the
present time wish to know it thoroughly, as a rule
proceed there to learn it. The Druids are wont to
hold aloof from war, and pay no taxes, being thus
free from military service and civil duties. Under
the inducement of such great rewards, many come
themselves into their ranks, or are sent by their
parents and friends. With them they learn off a
great number of lines of poetry, so that some remain
under training for twenty years. And they do
not regard it allowable by divine laws to commit
these things to writing, though in secular matters
they use Greek letters. The reason for this seems

to be twofold, that they do not wish either their
system to be made public, or their pupils to fail to
cultivate their memory by trusting to writing, as
generally happens when books can be resorted to.
Their chief doctrine is that souls do not perish, but
pass after death from one individual to another,
and this—the removal of the fear of death—they
think the greatest incitement to valour. They
theorise largely on astronomy, on the size of the
universe and the earth, on nature, and on the power
and might of the gods, and in these matters they
instruct the youth. Cæsar further on tells that the
Druids presided at the human sacrifices, and in the
7th book he gives us to know that the Æduan
magistrates, at least, were elected by them. Cicero,
in his treatise on " Divination," written a few years
later, introduces his brother Quintus as saying :
" The principles of divination are not overlooked
among barbarous nations even, as, for instance, in
Gaul there are the Druids, one of whom Divitiacus,
the Æduan, I knew ; he was a guest of yours and
great in your praises. He professed to know natural
philosophy, which the Greeks call ' physiology,'
and he used to tell partly by augury, partly by
conjecture, what was to happen in the future."
Cicero's contemporary, Diodorus Siculus, tells
us that among the Gauls were bards, certain
philosophers and divines named Druids, and soothsayers, adding that " the system of Pythagoras
held sway among them," that is, the doctrine of the

transmigration of souls. To this doctrine Varelius Maximus refers when he says : " One would have laughed at these long-trousered philosophers [the Druids], if we had not found their doctrine under the cloak of Pythagoras." Strabo, his contemporary in the first century of our era, gives us a short account of the Druids, half of which is but a variation of Cæsar's sketch. " Amongst the Gauls," he says, " there are generally three divisions of men, especially reverenced, the Bards, the Vates, and the Druids. The bards composed and chanted hymns ; the Vates occupied themselves with the sacrifices and the study of nature ; while the Druids joined to the study of nature that of moral philosophy. The belief in their justice is so great that the decision both of public and private disputes is referred to them, and they have before now by their decision prevented battle. All cases of murder are particularly referred to them. When there are plenty of these they imagine there will be a plentiful harvest. Both these and the others [Bards and Vates] assert that the soul is indestructible and likewise the world, but that fire and water will one day have the mastery." And further on he says that without the Druids the Gauls never sacrifice.

Another geographer, Pomponius Mela, refers to the Druids, but adds nothing to our knowledge, merely echoing Cæsar's description. Lucan, who died in 65, has been quoted in the former section for the names of the Gaulish gods ; but he further

proceeds to describe, after a reference to the bards,
the barbarous rites of the Druids and their theology.
The passage is mostly an expansion of Cæsar's reference to the transmigration of souls, but the poet
beautifully brings out how " Pluto's gloomy reign "
is not the habitation of souls, but that—

> " Forth they fly immortal in their kind,
>   And other bodies in new worlds they find ;
>   Thus life for ever runs its endless race,
>   And like a line death but divides the space.
>   Thrive happy they beneath their northern skies,
>   Who that worst fear—the fear of death—despise ;
>   Hence they no cares for this frail being feel,
>   But rush undaunted on the pointed steel ;
>   Provoke approaching fate and bravely scorn
>   To spare that life which must so soon return."

The writer on the Druids, next in importance to
Cæsar, is Pliny the Elder. He has several interesting
allusions to them and their superstitions. At the
end of his 16th book he mentions the admiration
of the Gauls for the mistletoe. " The Druids," he
says " (for so they name their *magi*) hold nothing
more sacred than the mistletoe, and the tree on which
it grows, provided it be the oak. They choose
groves of that tree, and conduct no sacrifice without
a garland of its leaves, so that we may possibly
suppose the Druids are so called from its Greek
name [*drus*]. Whatever grows on the oak is considered a gift from heaven." And he proceeds to
tell how it was culled from the tree, as has already
been told. Pliny mentions other plant superstitions

of the Gauls, connecting the rites naturally enough
with the Druids who presided. The next important *fetish* he mentions is the club-moss (selago) ;
it must be touched by no metal, but plucked by the
right hand passed through the tunic under the left,
with a thievish gesture ; the worshipper must be
dressed in white, with feet washed and bare ; and
the plant must be carried in a new cloth.   The Druids
held that it was a charm against all misfortunes,
and the smoke of its burning leaves cured diseases
of the eye.   In much the same way they thought
the " samolus," or water pimpernel, a talisman
against murrain in cattle. Vervain was another
plant, " about which the Gaulish *magi* raged,"
which cured everything, and had to be gathered
at the rise of the dog-star, and when neither sun nor
moon was seen. But these plant superstitions
and ceremonies have nothing especially " Druidic "
about them ; they are common among other nations
as well. Pliny's account of the serpent's egg—
the *anguinum*—is more important and special.
The snake's egg was said to be produced from the
frothy sweat of a number of serpents writhing in an
entangled mass, and to be tossed up into the air
as soon as formed. The Druid who was fortunate
enough to catch it in his cloak as it fell rode off at
full speed, pursued by the serpents, until stopped by
a running stream. If tried, the egg would swim
in water though cased in gold. Pliny says he saw
one himself, " about the size of a moderately large

apple, with a cartilaginous rind, studded with cavities like the arms of a polypus." A Roman knight was making use of it in court to gain an unfair verdict, and for this was put to death by Claudius the Emperor. And, lastly, in speaking of magic and its " vanities," he says that " Britain celebrates them to-day with such ceremonies that it might seem possible that she taught magic to the Persians," and " Gaul was overrun with magic arts even up to our own time, until Tiberius Cæsar did away with the Druids and this class of prophets and medicine-men." This passage has puzzled many commentators, for if the Druids were done away with, how does Pliny elsewhere mention them as still existent in Gaul ? And to add to the difficulty, Suetonius, a generation later, says that " Claudius abolished entirely the religion of the Druids, a religion of dreadful barbarity, and forbidden only the Roman citizens under Augustus." Pliny and Suetonius do not agree as to which Emperor abolished Druidism, nor can we well believe that it was altogether abolished even then : it would appear that only the human sacrifices and certain modes of divination were put a stop to. Strabo, indeed, says as much ; and we can see from Tacitus that the prophecies of the Druids incurred political wrath as late as Vespasian's time—after the abolition of Druidism, according to Pliny. Human sacrifices and, probably, meddling in politics were sure to bring the wrath of Rome on the system. Tacitus gives us an insight of how at times the Romans did put a stop to these phases of Druidism. In describing the attack of the Romans on Mona, or Anglesea, he represents the legions as awe-struck by the appearance of the Druids amid their opponents' ranks, pouring curses and vengeance on their heads, with hands upraised to heaven. But they were rolled in their own fires, and the groves sacred to grim superstitions were cut down ; " for," he adds, " they hold it lawful to sacrifice captives at their altars and to consult the gods from the movements of human entrails." After the first century, writers speak of Druidism as a thing of the past ; evidently the decrees of the Emperors had done away with its fiercer elements of superstition, and the purer and more philosophical parts had been absorbed into the usual Roman faith. Christianity, at least, had no contest with Druidism either in Gaul or in England. It may be mentioned that Amminaus Marcellinus, in the fourth century, gives us a few lines on the old and long extinct Druidism. After noticing the foundation of Marseilles by a Phocean colony, he says that when the people in those parts got gradually civilised, the learned studies which had been begun by the bards, the Euhages (probably a corruption of Vates) and the Druids, throve vigorously. Of these, he says, the Druids were the intellectual superiors of the others, and were formed into unions in accordance with the precepts of Pythagoras, where deep and hidden problems were discussed, and looking from a lofty philosophic pinnacle on human affairs, they pronounced human souls immortal.

Such is the history of Druidism in Gaul and early Britain : of its course in Ireland we have no direct information. It is only when Christianity has been long established, and Druidism a thing of the remote past, that we have writers who speak of the Druids ; and in their eyes the Druids were but magicians that attended the courts of the pagan kings. The lives of the pioneer saints, Patrick and Columba, are full of contests between themselves and the royal magicians, who are called in the Gaelic *Druid* and in the Latin versions *Magi*. But in all the numerous references to them in Irish chronicles and tales there is no hint given of Druidism being either a system of philosophy or religion : the Druids of Irish story are mere magicians and diviners, sometimes only conjurors. But as such—as magicians—the Druids play a most important part in Irish pagan history, as chronicled by the long posterior Christian writers. From the primæval landing of Partholan with his three Druids, to the days of Columba, we have themselves and the bards exercising magic and divining powers. The second fabled settlers of Ireland, the Nemedians, meet the invading Fomorians with magic spells ; but the fairy host of the Tuatha De Dannan are *par excellence* the masters of Druidic art. Their power over the forces of Nature—over sea, wind, and storms—shows them

plainly to be only degraded gods, who allow the sons
of Miled to land after showing them their power
and sovereignty as deities over the island. The
kings and chiefs had Druids about them to interpret
omens and to work spells ; but there is no reference
to these Druids being a priestly class, and their power
was limited to the functions of mere divination and
sorcery. Two of the most famous Druids were
Cathbadh, Druid of Conchobar Mac Nessa, the
instructor of Cuchulain, who, among many other
things, foretells the fate of Deirdre and the sons
of Uisnach, even before Deirdre was born ; and
Mogh Ruith of Munster, who single-handed opposed
Cormac and his Druids, and drove them by his
magic fire and storm-spells out of Munster. The
Druids of King Loegaire oppose St. Patrick with
their magic arts ; one of them causes snow to fall
so thickly that men soon find themselves neck-deep
in it, and at another time he brings over the land an
Egyptian darkness that might be felt. But the saint
defeats them, even on their own ground, much as
Moses defeats the Egyptian magicians. St. Columba,
in Adamnan's life of him, is similarly represented as
overcoming the spells of the northern Druids.
Broichan, Druid to King Brude, caused such a storm
and darkness on Loch-Ness that the navigation
appeared impossible, until the saint gave orders
that the sails should be unfurled and a start made.
Then everything became calm and settled. We are
also told in many instances how the Druids worked

these spells. A wisp of hay, over which an incantation was made, when cast on a person, caused idiocy and deformity. The Druidic wand plays an important part, a blow from it causing transformations and spells. It must be remarked, too, that the wood used for wands and Druidic rites and fires was not the oak at all, as in Gaul: sacred wood among the Irish Druids would appear to have been the yew, hawthorn, and, more especially, the rowan tree. Divination was an important feature of Druidic accomplishments, and there were various forms of it. Pure Druidic divination sometimes consisted in watching the Druidic fire—how the smoke and flame went. Sometimes the Druid would chew a bit of raw flesh with incantation or " oration " and an invocation to the gods, and then generally the future was revealed to him. Sometimes, if this failed, he had to place his two hands upon his two cheeks and fall into a divine sleep, a method known as " illumination by the palms of the hands." Fionn used to chew his thumb when he wanted any supernatural knowledge. The bards, too, were diviners at times, a fact that would appear to show their ancient connection with the Druids. The bardic divination is known as " illumination by rhymes," when the bard in an ecstatic state pours forth a flood of poetry, at the end of which he brings out the particular fact that is required to be known. Connected with this is the power of poetic satire. If a man refused a gift, the bard could

satirise him in such a way that personal injury
would result, such as blisters and deformities.

Irish Druidism consists, therefore, merely of magic
and divination ; it is not a philosophy, nor a religion,
nor a system.   It is quite true that we have, at least,
an echo now and then of the time when Druidism
in Ireland and Scotland was something different,
and when even human sacrifices were offered.
Columba, in commencing the building of his church
at Iona, addressed his followers in words which
clearly point to human sacrifice. " It is good for
us," says he, " that our roots should go under the
earth here ; it is permitted that one of you should go
under the clay of this island to hallow it." The
story goes on to say that Odran arose readily, and
spoke thus : " If thou shouldst take me, I am ready
for that." Columba readily accepted his offer,
and " then Odran went to heaven, and Columba
founded the church of Hi."   It is said that a human
being was slain at the foundation of Emain, the
mythic capital of Ulster ; and in Nennius we have
a remarkable story told of King Vortigern.   He was
trying to build a castle on Snowdon, but somehow,
though he gathered ever so much material, every
time it was " spirited " away during the night.
He sought counsel from his " magi " (the Irish
translation calls them Druids), and they told him
that he must find a child born without a father,
and must put him to death, and sprinkle with his
blood the ground where the castle was to stand.

Nor is tradition of the present time silent on this matter. It is said that Tigh-a-chnuic, Kilcoy, in the Black Isle, had its foundation consecrated by the slaughter of a stranger who chanced to be passing when the house was to be built, but unfortunately his ghost used to haunt the house until he was able to disburden his woes to somebody, and he then disappeared.

The sum and result of our inquiry into Druidism may be given in the words of Professor Rhys :— " At the time of Cæsar's invasions, they were a powerful class of men, monopolizing the influence of soothsayers, magicians, and priests. But in Gaul, under the faint rays of the civilization of Marseilles and other Mediterranean centres, they seem to have added to their other characters that of philosophers, discoursing to the youths, whose education was entrusted to them, on the stars and their movements, on the world and its countries, on the nature of things, and the power of the gods." Whether the doctrine of the transmigration of souls was really of native origin or borrowed from the Greeks, must remain an open question. Some think it unlikely that the central doctrine of Druidism should have been derived so late in the history of the nation, or derived at all, from a foreign source, and they appeal to the fact that Britain was the home of Druidism, a country which could have had little intercourse with Marseilles. But in connection with this idea of its British origin, it must be re-

membered that at a certain stage of culture, nations
are apt to consider their neighbours, provided they
are in a lower stage of civilization, much more
religious than themselves. The Romans always
believed the Etrurians to be more versed in religious
matters than themselves. So, too, the Gauls probably looked on British Druidism, with its " pristine
grimness " of practices, as the source of their own,
while in reality their own was doubtless an independent but more enlightened development. Professor Rhys considers Druidism to be of a non-Aryan
character, and calls it the religion of the pre-Celtic
tribes, from the Baltic to Gibraltar. Now, in what
we have left us recorded of Druidism there is ab-
solutely nothing that can be pointed to as non-Aryan.
The strong priestly caste presented to us in Cæsar,
as divided off from the nobles and the commons,
can be somewhat paralleled in the Hinduism of
India with its rigidly priestly caste of Brahmans,
who monopolised all religious rites. And Brah-
manism is an Aryan religion. Among the Gauls,
from the superstitious cast of their minds, a priestly
class was sure to arise to a position of supreme
power. Their human sacrifices can be matched,
in some degree, by actual instances of such, and by
rites which pointed to them as previously existent,
among other Aryan nations, including those of
Greece and Rome ; only here, as before, the im-
pressionable and superstitious character of the
Gauls drove them to greater excesses. The doctrine

of the transmigration of the soul is a tenet of both Brahmans and Buddhists, of Aryan India, and it found its classical development in the views of the Greek Pythagoras. The position and fame of the Druids as magicians is, as Pliny points out, of the same nature as those of the Magi of Aryan Persia. Some again think it absurd that if the Druids were such philosophers, as they are represented to have been, they would be so superstitious as to practise human sacrifices, and other wild rites. But there is no incongruity in at once being philosophic and superstitious ; the human mind is very hospitable in its entertainment of quite opposite opinions, especially in moral and religious matters ; for there is a wide difference between theories of the intellect and practices prompted by the emotions.

CELTIC RELIGION IN BRITAIN AND IRELAND.

In tracing the history of Celtic religion, we have established that the religion of the Gauls fully represents the pagan religion of both the great branches of the Celtic race—the Brythonic (Gauls and Welsh) and the Goidelic (Gaelic races). From Cæsar's account of the religion of the Gauls to the first native notices of even the history of Celtic Britain and Ireland, there is practically a period of a thousand years. During the interval, Chris-

tianity had established its sway, nominally at least,
over the whole land, and paganism was for centuries
a thing of the past.   It may, however, be remarked
that one or two Latin ecclesiastic al histories appeared
in the eighth century—notably the works of Adamnan
and Bede, but we in vain scan the pages left us of
their works for any definite information as to the
previous religion.   Gildas, a century before either
of these writers, makes only a passing reference to
the old faith.   " I shall not," says he, " enumerate
those diabolical idols of my country, which almost
surpassed in number those of Egypt, and of which
we still see [circ. A.D. 560] some mouldering away
within or without the deserted temples, with stiff
and deformed features as was customary.   Nor will
I call out upon the mountains, fountains, or hills,
or upon the rivers, which now are subservient to the
use of men, but once were an abomination and
destruction to them, and to which the blind people
paid divine honour."   Our knowledge of the local
development of Celtic religion in Britain and Ireland
cannot be obtained directly from contemporary
history : we have, it is true, some British inscriptions
of the Roman period, which give, mid a host of
minor and local deities, one or two important gods.
But our information must be drawn, nearly all,
from the heroic poems and tales, which do not date
much earlier than a thousand years ago ; and most
are far later than this period.   For information
as to the ritual of the old religion, local customs

and superstitions—Beltaine bannocks and Samhuinn fires—form our only guides.

It will also be necessary to discuss separately the remains of the religion of the early Welsh and the early Gaels. The religion of the former we shall name " British," of the latter, " Gaelic." And it must be remembered that the Welsh are doubtless the remnant of the Gaulish population which, about the time of the Roman conquest, must have occupied England (except Cornwall and Wales) and Lowland Scotland. Gaul and England had, therefore, practically the same people and language in the first century of this era, and there now remain of them still speaking the language, the Bretons of France and the Welsh of Wales, from which country they drove out or absorbed the previous Gaelic population in the fifth century of our era, or thereabouts. The " Gaelic Religion " will include the early religion of Ireland and the Highlands of Scotland.

BRITISH RELIGION.

The gods of Britain suffered what appears to have been the " common lot " of gods ; they were changed into the kings and champions, the giants and enchanters, of heroic tales and folk-lore. In the words of the poet :—

" Ye are gods, and behold ye shall die, and the waves be upon you
     at last.
 In the darkness of time, in the deeps of the years, in the changes
     of things,
 Ye shall sleep as a slain man sleeps, and the world shall forget
     you for kings."

The great deity, " Belinus," appears in the pages of
Geoffrey of Monmouth, as a mere mortal conqueror.
In company with his brother, Brennus or " Bran,"
he marched to the siege of Rome, when " Gabius
and Porsena " were consuls ! Gargantua appears
twice as a British King, under the title of Gurgiunt.
Camulus, the war-god, who gave his name to
Camulodunum, now *Col*-chester, is presented as
Coel Hen, " Old King Coul " of the song, who gave
his name to the Aryshire district of Kyle.   The god,
" Nodens," is the Nudd of Welsh, and King Nuada,
of Irish story ; and Lir, the sea-god, is immortalised
in the pages of Shakespeare as an old British king,
Some of the gods fight under Arthur's banner, and
perish on the battlefield of Camlan, along with him.
There, is, consequently, a considerable amount of
confusion in the Welsh tales, which does not appear
in the more consistent tales of Ireland.   Probably,
there were kings of the names of Beli, Coel, Urien,
and Arthur, and there certainly were kings and
chiefs, of the names of Brennus, Cassibelaunus,
and Caractacus, but their history is irretrievably
mixed up with that of deities and demigods, possessed
of similar names.   Thus, Bran the Blessed, is a son
of Lir, a personage of such gigantic proportions
that no house could hold him, and evidently a
degraded god, possibly a war-god.   He next appears
as father of Caradoc, for whom he is sent as hostage
to Rome, when the latter is conquered by Claudius.
In Rome he is converted to Christianity, which he

introduced into Britain, and hence his name of
" Bran the Blessed." And again he is brother of
Belinus, and the same as the Brennus of the Roman
historians, who sacked Rome in B.C. 390. It is,
therefore, a matter of great difficulty to take either
history or myth out of the confusion in Welsh poetry
and tradition, caused by a little knowledge of
classical and Biblical history, a history which is
interwoven with native myths and facts.

The inscriptions of Roman times show that the
religious condition of Britain then differed in no
respect from that of Gaul. The local deities were
assimilated to the corresponding deities of Rome,
and we have in Britain combinations like those
met with in Gaul : the Roman deity has the corresponding British name attached to him on the votive
inscription by way of epithet. Thus, at Bath, altars
are dedicated to Sul-Minerva, Sul being a goddess
unknown elsewhere. On the Roman wall, between
the Forth and Clyde, the name of Mars-Camulus
appears on the inscriptions, among many others
to the " genii " of the places, the spirits of " the
mountain and the flood," and to " Sancta Britannia "
and " Brigantia," the goddesses of Britain and the
land of the Brigantes respectively. The most
interesting inscriptions were those found in the
temple of a god discovered at Lydney Park, in
Gloucestershire. One inscription bears to be to the
" great god Nodon," which proves the temple to
have been dedicated to the worship of Nodon, a

god of the deep sea, figured on a bronze plaque as a Triton or Neptune borne by sea-horses and surrounded by a laughing crowd of Nereids. This deity is identified with the legendary Nudd, known in Welsh fiction only as the father of famous sons and in Irish story as King Nuada of the Silver Hand, who fought the two battles of Moytura, and fell in the second before " Balor of the Evil Eye," the King of the Fomorians.

Passing, however, to the Welsh legends and myths preserved in the " Ancient Books of Wales " and in the prose " Mabinogion," we can easily eliminate three principal families of deities, the children of " Don," of " Nudd," and of " Lir." Of these the first are purely Welsh, the second—the children of Nudd—have Irish equivalents both in name and office, while the children of Lir belong equally to both nations. The family of Don is evidently connected with the sky and its changes. He has given his name in Welsh to the constellation of Cassiopeia, called Llys Don, the court of Don. The milky way is named after his son, Gwydion, Caer Gwydion, the city of Gwydion ; and his daughter Arianrhod, " silver-circled," inhabits the bright circle of stars which is called the Northern Crown. With the name Don may be compared that of the father of the Irish hero Diarmat, son of Donn. Gwydion is the greatest of enchanters—a prince of the powers of the air. He can change the forms of trees, men, and animals, and along with " Math, the son of Mathonwy," his master, styled by Professor Rhys, the Cambrian Pluto, though rather a god of air than earth, he forms a woman out of flowers. "They took the blossoms of the oak, and the blossoms of the broom, and the blossoms of the meadow-sweet, and produced from them a maiden, the fairest and most graceful that man ever saw." Amaethon, the son of Don, is a husbandman—doubtless a god of weather and crops. He has a fight with Arawn, king of Annwn, or Hell, for a white roebuck and a whelp, which he had carried off from the realms of darkness. The battle is known as the "battle of the trees," and in it Gywdion, by his divinations, won the victory for his brother, for he guessed the name of the person in the ranks of his opponents, which had to be guessed before either side won.

Nudd, like Don, is eclipsed by his family. He appears to have been god of the deep and its treasures. His son Gwynn, known always as Gwynn ap Nudd, is the Welsh king of the Fairies in the widest sense of the word. It would appear that Gwynn is no less a person than the god of the next world for human beings. He answers, therefore, to the king of "Tir-nan-og," "Land of Youth" of the Irish legends, and "Tir-fo-Thuinn" of the Gaelic stories— the land below the waves. The son of the deep-sea god is naturally enough made lord over the happy realm under the waves of the west. Christian bias, however, gave Gwynn a more sinister position.

We are told that God placed him over the brood
of devils in Annwn, lest they should destroy the
present race. A Saint of the name of Collen one
day heard two men conversing about Gwynn ap
Nudd, and saying that he was King of Annwn and
the fairies. " Hold your tongue quickly," says
Collen, " these are but devils." " Hold thou thy
tongue," said they, " thou shalt receive a reproof
from him." And sure enough the Saint was summoned to the palace of Gwynn on a neighbouring
hill top, where he was kindly received, and bid
sit down to a sumptuous repast. " I will not eat
the leaves of the trees," said Collen ; for he saw
through the enchantments of Gwynn, and, by the
use of some holy water, caused Gwynn and his
castle to disappear in the twinkling of an eye. The
story is interesting, as showing how the early mission-
aries dealt with the native gods. Gwynn, according
to St. Collen, is merely a demon. His connection
with the lower world is brought out by his fight
with Gwythyr, the son of Greidwal, for Cordelia,
the daughter of Lir or Lud. She is represented
as a splendid maiden, daughter of the sea-god Lir,
" a blossom of flowering seas," at once a Venus
and a Proserpine, goddess of the summer flowers,
for whom there is a fight between the powers of the
worlds above and below the earth respectively.
Peace was made between these two deities on these
these conditions : " that the maiden should remain
in her father's house, without advantage to either

of them, and that Gwynn ap Nudd, and Gwythyr,
the son of Greidwal, should fight for her every first
of May, from thenceforth till the day of doom, and
that whichever of them should be conqueror then,
should have the maiden."

We have thus discovered in Don and his children
the powers of sky and air, answering to Jove and
his Olympians of Classical Mythology : in Nudd
and his son Gwynn we have probably found the
powers that rule over the land of " shades," corresponding to Pluto or Dis ; and we now come to
consider the third family of British deities, Lir and
his children, whom we shall find to be the British
and Gaelic equivalents of Neptune, the sea-god,
and Aphrodite, " daughter of the foam." Lir,
or as the Welsh spell the name, Llyr, is the same as
the Gaelic *lear*, found in the Ossianic poems, and
signifying the " sea." Lir is therefore the personification of the sea—the sea deified. He is a deity
common to both Britons and Gaels ; indeed, it may
rather be said that he is more properly a deity of
the Gaels transferred into the British pantheon.
The epithet *Llediaith*, or " half-speech," that is,
" dialect," which is attached to his name, goes to
show that he was not a deity of native British origin.
We are therefore justified in considering Lir as the
sea deity of the ancient remnant of the Gaels still
surviving and maintaining their ground in Wales
in the fifth century, and represented as then expelled
by Cunedda and his sons. They were, however,

more probably slowly absorbed by the Welsh, who were then pressed westwards by the Saxons. All the legends preserved in Welsh, connected with Lir and his family, point to a strong Gaelic influence, if not to a Gaelic origin. Of Lir himself nothing is said in the Welsh legends beyond his being the father of so many children ; in Ireland he is represented as striving for the sovereignty of the Tuatha-De-Dannan, the Gaelic gods, with Bove Derg, son of the Dagda, and, when defeated in his aspirations, as retiring to Sidh-Fionnachaidh. Here he leads the life of a provincial chief, and all else that we know of him is the cruel transformation of his four children by their wicked aunt and stepmother. Lir has also another name ; at least he must have had another name, or else Manannan, his son, and Cordelia, his daughter, must each have had two fathers. In some traditions they are both represented as the children of Llud. The same confusion, of course, appears in the Irish genealogy of Mannanan ; for the most part he is known as the son of Lir, but in the genealogies he is set down as the son of Alloid, doubtless the original, or, at least, the equivalent of Llud. Professor Rhys thinks that Llud stands for Nudd, the N changing into Ll, because Llud also received the title of Llaw Ereint, "silver-handed," just as the Irish King Nuada did ; and the principle of alliteration required the changing of Nudd Llaw Ereint into Llud Llaw Ereint. And Nudd, besides, was somehow a god of the sea ;

what was the necessity of two chief sea-gods ?   We
have interpreted Nudd as a god of the " land under
the waves," and not as the sea-god proper ; and,
again, the Irish Alloid is distinctly against any
such change of letters as Nudd into Llud, besides
its being otherwise far from probable that such a
change should occur on any principle of alliteration.
Lir, under the name of Llud, is, in the histories
and tales the brother of Cassibelaunus, Cæsar's
opponent, and in his reign Britain was troubled with
three direful plagues : the Coranians, a people
" whose knowledge was such that there was no
discourse upon the face of the Island, however it
might be spoken, but what, if the wind blew it, it
was known to them ; " second, a shriek that occurred every May eve, that created all kinds of
terrors and horrors ; and, third, the king's winter
provisions disappeared every year when stored.
From these plagues the wisdom of his brother
Llevelys freed King Llud.   Lir appears in the pages
of Geoffrey of Monmouth as an old British king,
who reigned long before Llud, and who had three
daughters, whose story forms the groundwork of
Shakespeare's tragedy of King Lear.

Manannan, the son of Lir, is in the Welsh Myths
one of the seven—that mystical number, so common
in the old Welsh poems—who escaped from Ireland
on the death of his brother, Bran, the blessed, king
of Britain.   Returning with the head of Bran, the
seven heroes found the throne usurped by Cassibel-

aunus and retired to Harlech, where the birds of Rhiannon kept them enchanted by their music for seven years ; and after this they feasted for eighty years more at Gwales in Penvro, from which place they set out to London and buried Bran's head with its face to France. As long as Bran's head was left there facing France no invasion of Britain could be successful. Unfortunately Arthur exhumed the head, declaring that he would maintain the country against any foe without need of supernatural safeguard. In his subsequent career Manannan is seen to be a deity who presides over arts and commerce, a god who is " deep in counsel." He and another of the mythic seven wander about doing artificers' work ; he successively tries saddle-making, shoe-making, and shieldmaking, trades in which he outdistances all competitors as a matter of course. From the Irish accounts of him, Manannan Mac Lir, appears to be a god of sea and wind. Cormac, Archbishop of Cashel, of the ninth century, describes him in his glossary like a true Euhemerist, as " *Manannan mac lir*, a renowned trader who dwelt in the Island of Man. He was the best pilot in the west of Europe. Through acquaintance with the sky he knew the quarter in which would be fair weather and foul weather, and when each of these two seasons would change. Hence the Scots and the Britons called him a god of the sea, and hence they said he was son of the sea, that is, *mac lir*, ' son of the sea.' " Manannan is otherwise represented as one of the

Tuatha-De-Dannan chiefs. He was the possessor
of that wonderful steed mentioned in the story of
the " children of Tuireann." Luga of the Long
Arms " rode the steed of Manannan Mac Lir, namely
Enbarr of the Flowing Mane : no warrior was ever
killed on the back of this steed, for she was as swift
as the cold clear wind of spring, and she travelled
with equal ease on land and on sea. He wore Manannan's coat of mail ; no one could be wounded
through it, or above it or below it. He had on his
breast Manannan's breast-plate, which no weapon
could pierce. Manannan's sword, The Answerer,
hung at his left side ; no one ever recovered from its
wound ; and those who were opposed to it in the
battle-field were so terrified by looking at it that
their strength left them and they became weaker
than women." In the curious story called the
" Sick-bed of Cuchulainn," Manannan is represented
as a fairy chief who deserts his fairy bride Fand,
but Fand is helped and loved by Cuchulainn, mortal
though he was. Manannan on discovering this,
returns to his wife and shakes his magic cloak between
her and Cuchulainn," so that they should never
meet again. This magic cloak had also the effect
of producing forgetfulness of the past. Of Manannan, Mr. Elton says : " In him we see personified
the splendour and swiftness of the sun ; the god
rushes over the waves like a ' wheel of fire ' and his
three-legged shape recalls the giant strides of Vishnu.
He was the patron of traffic and merchandise. The

best weapons and jewels from across the sea were thought to be gifts from the god."

Branwen, "white-bosom," the daughter of Lir, is the central figure of the most tragic of Welsh myths. She is married to Matholwch, King of Ireland, who treats her badly. Her brother Bran, coming to know of it, invades Ireland. The Irish yield, and build a house big enough for Bran to enter into, a thing he never hitherto could get, so enormous was his size. But the Irish had decided to murder their guests at the first feast in the great house. The cleverness of one of Bran's men foils their purpose ; there is, however, a general slaughter, in which the Irish have at first the best of it, for they possess a cauldron, into which, when any one is dipped that is dead, he comes to life hale and sound. But the cauldron is discovered by the already-mentioned one of Bran's men, and he breaks it. Bran is killed, and only seven return of his people to Wales. The story as a whole is a very widely-spread one ; it appears in about a dozen forms in Teutonic lands— the Volsung Saga and the Nibelung story being the most famous forms of it. Probably there are in the myth the evidences of a time when Celt and Teuton lived not too amicably together on the banks of the Rhine, a supposition which would obviate the necessity of supposing the Celtic version a borrowed one, inferior though it may be in some details. Another legend represents Branwen or Brangwaine as helping the loves, illicit though they

be, of Tristram and Iseult. It is she that hands to
Tristram the fateful love-potion which binds him
irrevocably to Iseult. Hence Mr. Elton considers
her the Venus of the Northern Seas. Indeed the
sea was poetically named " the fountain of Venus,"
according to the Iolo MSS. ; and a verse in the
" Black Book of Carmarthen " gives this stanza :—

> " Accursed be the damsel
> Who, after the wailing,
> Let loose the Fountain of Venus, the raging deep."

From this we can easily understand how Branwen
may be Venus and daughter of the sea-god as well,
just as Aphrodite was sprung from the foam of the
sea. Cordelia, another daughter of Lear or Llud,
has already been mentioned as the resplendent
summer goddess for whom the powers of air and the
shades fight every May-day till the day of doom.

In the remarkable Mabinogi entitled " Kilhwch
and Olwen," so full of mythologic lore, we can see
the true character of at least one of Arthur's knights.
This is his seneschal Kai. From the references
in this mythic tale, it could alone be proved that
Kai was no less than the British Vulcan, the fire-god.
" Kai," says the tale, " had this peculiarity, that
his breath lasted nine nights and nine days under
water, and he could exist nine days and nine nights
without sleep. A wound from Kai's sword no
physician could heal. Very subtle was Kai. When
it pleased him he could render himself as tall as the
highest tree in the forest. And he had another

peculiarity : so great was the heat of his nature
that when it rained hardest, whatever he carried
remained dry for a handbreadth above and a handbreadth below his hand ; and when his companions
were coldest he was to them as fuel with which to
light their fire." Such was Arthur's steward !
Hephaestus and Vulcan do equally mean duties
in the halls of Olympus. The gods laugh heartily
at the limping gait and ungainly appearance of
Hephaestus as he hands round the cup of nectar.
So is Kai often the butt of Arthur's knights. Another
of Arthur's knights may be mentioned as probably
a degraded war deity. Owain, the son of Urien
Rheged, is never mentioned in the older poems and
tales without reference to his army of ravens, " which
rose as he waved his wand, and swept men into
the air and dropped them piecemeal on the ground."
We are here reminded of the Irish war goddess who
so often appears as, and is indeed named, the " scald-
crow " (*Badb*). Odin, too, has his ravens to consult
with, and to act as his messengers. Many others
of Arthur's heroes partake of the same mythical
type ; of Arthur himself we shall speak again in
considering the Celtic hero-tales. At present, it
is sufficient to say that Arthur is, at least, as mythical
as any of the rest we have mentioned.

Nor must we overlook Caridwen, who is considered
even by the Welsh themselves, their goddess of
nature. She is possessed of a cauldron of " inspir-
ation and science," which, as Mr. Nutt points out,

may be regarded as a symbol of the reproductive power of the earth. It is doubtless this same cauldron that has appeared in the story of Branwen the daughter of Lir : when the dead heroes were plunged into it they were resuscitated. The Tuatha-De-Dannan were possessed in Scythia of a similar cauldron, similarly employed. Caridwen, the tale says, set her cauldron to boil, and placed Gwion Bach, the dwarf, and the blind Morda to watch it, charging them not to suffer it to cease boiling for a year and a day. Towards the end of the year, three drops of the boiling liquor spluttered out upon the hand of Gwion, and suddenly putting his hand in his mouth because of the heat, the future and present were revealed to him. The cauldron burst, the fairy returned, and Gwion had to run for his life. Pursued at once by Caridwen, he changed himself into a hare and fled. But she changed herself into a greyhound and turned him. And he ran towards the river and became a fish ; she took the form of an otter and gave chase. He then became a bird, and she a hawk, and as she was swooping down upon him he fell among a heap of wheat and became one of the grains. She, however, became a high-crested black hen, scratched the heap, found him, and swallowed him. He was thereafter born as a beautiful boy, whom Caridwen had not the heart to kill. She put him in a leather sack, and cast him into the sea. Being washed ashore, he was discovered, and brought to Prince Elphin, to whom he immediately, child though he was, began to sing most elegant poetry. This youthful poet was none else than Taliesin, "prince of song, and the chief of the bards of the west." The poems ascribed to Taliesin have been called the romance of metempsychosis. "The Druidical doctrine of the trans- migration of souls is thought to be hidden in the poet's account of his wonderful transformations." A specimen or two out of many such may be quoted.—

> " I have been in a multitude of shapes,
> Before I assumed a consistent form,
> I have been a sword narrow, variegated,
> I have been a tear in the air ;
> I have been the dullest of stars,
> I have been a word among letters,
> I have been a book in the origin."

And again—

> " I have been a sow, I have been a buck,
> I have been a sage, I have been a snout,
> I have been a horn, I have been a wild sow,
> I have been a shout in battle."

Evidently there is in these poems of Taliesin the broken-down remembrance of the old Druidic cult. True enough the poet does show a wonderful and suspicious acquaintance with the " Metamorphoses " of Ovid and his account of Pythagorean doctrines, as he also does with even Irish mythology, for he speaks of his place in Caer *Sidi*, doubtless the Irish *Side*, thus—

> " Complete is my chair in Caer Sidi,
> No one will be afflicted with disease or old age that may be in it."

Yet for all this, for all his mingling of Greek, Roman,
and Jewish history and myth, we may believe that
there is at bottom a germ of genuine Druidic influence, and of genuine Welsh myth. As a matter
of fact, the tale of the cauldron appears in the history
of the Gaelic counterpart of Taliesin—in the closing
scenes of Ossian's career, and not at the beginning,
as in Taliesin's case. Ossian, old and blind, tried
to recover his youth by magical means. He now
lived among little men who could not give him
food enough, and consequently he had a belt round
his waist with three skewers—*dealg*—in it to tighten
his stomach. He went out one day with his gillie
to hunt, and by some supernatural means brought
down three remarkable deer. These he took home
and put in a cauldron to be cooked, bidding his gillie
watch them, and on no account to taste any of the
food. All went right for a time ; the deer were
cooked ; Ossian ate the first and let out one
shewer ; he ate a second and let out a second skewer ;
but as misfortune would have it, while the third
deer was simmering in the cauldron a drop of the
broth spurted out on the gillie's hand, which he
instantly put into his mouth. Ossian ate the third
deer and let out the third skewer, but no youth
returned to him. The licking of the little drop of
broth had broken the spell. The supernatural
knowledge and power gained by Gwion Bach do not,
of course, appear in this tale, but it may be observed
that Finn gained his knowledge of futurity in a

manner which, though dissimilar in details, is yet
the same in result. Following a strange woman
that he saw one day, he came to a hill side, where
she entered by a concealed door. Finn attempted
to follow her inside, and had his hand on the door-
post, when the door suddenly shut on him and
jammed his thumb. With difficulty extricating
his thumb, he very naturally shoved the hurt member
into his mouth, when lo ! he found himself possessed
of the gift of seeing future events. This gift, however, he possessed only when he bruised his thumb
in his mouth.

THE GAELIC GODS IN HISTORY.

Material for reconstructing the Olympus of the
Gaels is not at all so scanty as we have found it to
be in the case of the Welsh. There is, it is true,
no general description of the Irish Olympus, but
references to particular deities are not uncommon.
The earliest reference to any Irish gods occurs
in one of the oldest monuments we possess
of the Gaelic language ; a manuscript of the
St. Gall Monastery contains incantations to the
powers Diancecht and Goibniu. This manuscript
Zeuss sets down as of the eighth century, and it is,
therefore, eleven hundred years old. Cormac's
glossary, originally composed in the ninth century,
mentions as deities Art, Ana, Buanann, Brigit, Neit,

and Manannan. Keating quotes from the Book
of Invasions a poem that makes the Dagda " king
of heaven," and he further enumerates Badb, Macha,
and Morrighan as the three goddesses of the Tuatha-
de-Danann.   The Tuatha-de-Danann themselves
appear often in the tales as the fairy host, the *Side*
that dwell in the Land of Promise ; they interfere
in the affairs of mortals long after they are represented as having been expelled from Ireland, thus,
if not actually mentioned as having been the pagan
gods of the Gael, yet, despite the rampant Euhemer-
ism of Irish tales and histories, implicitly considered
as such.   And again, by adopting the same method
as in the case of the Welsh myths, we shall make the
Irish myths and histories, with their imposing array
of invasions and genealogies, deliver up the deities
they have consigned to the ranks of kings and heroes.

We must, however, first briefly indicate the leading
points of early Irish history, as set down in the
sober pages of their own annalists. Forty days
before the flood the Lady Caesair, granddaughter
of Noah, with fifty girls and three men, came to
Ireland. This is reckoned as the first " invasion "
or " taking " of Ireland. Of course she and her
company all perished when the flood came—all,
with one doubtful exception. For some legends,
with more patriotism than piety, represent Fionntan,
the husband of Caesair, as actually surviving the
flood. The way in which he accomplished this
feat is unlike that of the ancestor of the Macleans,

who weathered the flood in an ark of his own.   Fionntan, when the flood began, was cast into a deep sleep,
which continued for a year, and when he woke he
found himself in his own house at Dun-Tulcha, in
Kerry somewhere (for O'Curry has not been able
exactly to localise this important event).   He lived
here contemporaneously with the various dynasties
that ruled in Ireland down to the time of Dermot
in the sixth century of our era.   He then appears
for the last time, " with eighteen companies of his
descendants," in order to settle a boundary dispute,
since he was the oldest man in the world, and must
know all the facts.   This story is not believed in
by the more pious of the historians, for it too fla-
grantly contradicts the Scriptures.   It, therefore,
falls under O'Curry's category of " wild stories ; "
these are stories which contain some historic truth,
but are so overloaded with the fictions of the imagination as to be nearly valueless.   The Irish historians
have as much horror of a blank in their history,
as nature was once supposed to have of a vacuum.
The Lady Caesair fills the blank before the flood ;
Partholan and his colony fill the first blank after
the flood.   He came from Migdonia, the middle of
Greece, " twenty-two years before the birth of
Abraham," and was the ninth in descent from Noah,
all the intermediate names being duly given.   He
was not in the island ten years when the Fomorians,
or sea-rovers, disturbed him. These Fomorians
were a constant source of trouble to all succeeding

colonists, and sometimes they actually became
masters of the country. Some three hundred years
after their arrival, the colony of Partholan was cut
off by a plague. Plagues, and eruptions of lakes
and springs, fill up the gaps in the annals, when
genealogies and battles are not forthcoming. For
thirty years after the destruction of Partholan's
colony, Ireland was waste. Then came Nemed
and his sons, with their company, from " Scythia,"
in the year before Christ 2350. They were not long
in the Island when the Fomorians again appeared,
and began to harass the Nemedians. Both parties
were extremely skilled in Druidism, and they opposed
each other in a fierce contest of spells as well as
blows. The Fomorians were finally routed. Nemed
was the 12th in descent from Noah. He had four
sons—Starn, Jarbonnel, Fergus, and Aininn. Some
two hundred and sixteen years after coming to
Ireland, the Nemedians were overthrown by the
Fomorians and the plague together, and only thirty
escaped under the leadership of the three cousins,
grandsons of Nemed, Simeon Breac, son of Starn ;
Beothach, son of Jarbonnel ; and Britan Mael,
son of Fergus. Simeon Breac and his party went
to Greece, and after eleven generations returned
as the Firbolgs. Beothach, with his clan, went to
the northern parts of Europe, where they made
themselves perfect in the arts of Divination, Druidism, and Philosophy, and returned eleven generations later as the Tuatha-de-Danann. Britan Mael,

with his family, went to Mona, and from there poured
their descendants into the island, which is now
called Britain, after their leader, Britan Mael. The
Firbolgs, the descendants of Starn, son of Nemed,
being oppressed in Greece, much as the Israelites
were in Egypt, returned to Ireland, and took possession of it. " They were called the Firbolgs," we
are told, " from the bags of leather they used to have
in Greece for carrying soil to put on the bare rocks,
that they might make flowery plains under blossom
of them." The Firbolgs held Ireland for thirty-
six years, and then they were invaded by their
12th cousins, the Tuatha-de-Danann, the descendants
of Jarbonnel, son of Nemed.   Next to the Milesian
colony yet to come, the Tuatha-de-Danann are the
most important by far of the colonists, for in them
we shall by-and-bye discover the Irish gods.   What
the annalists tell of them is briefly this.   They came
from the north of Europe, bringing with them " four
precious jewels ; "   the first was the Lia Fail, the
Stone of Virtue or Fate, for wherever it was, there
a person of the race of Scots must reign ;   the sword
of Luga Lamfada ;   the spear of the same ;   and the
cauldron of the Dagda, from which " a company
never went away unsatisfied."   The Tuatha landed
in Ireland on the first of May, either 1900 or 1500
years before Christ, for the chronologies differ by
only a few hundred years.   They burned their ships
as a sign of " no retreat," and for three days concealed themselves in a mist of sorcery.   They then

demanded the Firbolgs to yield, which, however,
they would not do, and the great battle of Moytura
South was fought. The Firbolgs were routed with
immense slaughter. Nuada, leader of the Tuatha-
Dé in the battle, lost his hand in the fight, but Credne
Cerd, the artificer, made a silver one for him, and
Diancecht, the physician, fitted it on, while Miach,
his son, infused feeling and motion into every joint
and vein of it. For thirty years the Tuatha held
undisputed possession of Erin, but the Fomorians,
who were continually hovering about the coast,
now made a determined effort to conquer them.
The battle of Moytura North was fought between
them. In it Nuada of the Silver Hand fell, and so
did Balor of the Evil Eye, leader of the Fomorians.
He was slain by his grandson Luga of the Long Arms,
who was practically leader of the Tuatha, and who
succeeded to the kingship on the death of Nuada.
After a reign of forty years Luga died, and was
succeeded by the Dagda Mor, the central figure
of the Tuatha-de-Danann, and in the pages of our
Euhemerist annalists, an inscrutable and misty
personage. O'Curry ventures even to call him a
demigod. The Dagda was the twenty-fourth in
descent from Noah ; let it be observed that Nemid
was the twelfth in descent. The Firbolg chiefs also
were in the twenty-fourth generation from Noah.
Among the leading personages of the Tuatha were
Manannan, the son of Alloid or Lir ; Ogma, son of
Elathan, and brother of the Dagda, surnamed " Sur-

face ; " Goibniu, the smith ; Luchtine, the carpenter; Danann, mother of their gods ; Brigit, the poetess ; Badb, Macha, and Morrigan, " their three goddesses," says Keating. The Tuatha held Erin for nigh two hundred years, but when MacCuill, MacCecht, and MacGreine, who were so called " because Coll, Cecht, and Grian, the hazel, the plough, and the sun, were gods of worship to them," were ruling over Ireland with their respective queens Banba, Fodla, and Eire (three names of Ireland), the last colony of all appeared on the southern coast. These were the Milesians or Gaels from Spain and the East. They were in no respect related to the previous races, except that they were equally with them descended from Noah, Golam Miled, after whom they were called Milesians, being the twenty-fourth from Noah in direct descent. They were also called Gaels or Gaidels, from an ancestor Gadelus, seventh in descent from Noah, and son of Scota, daughter of Pharaoh. The family lived for the most part in Egypt, but Golam Miled, who was also married to a second Scota, daughter of Pharaoh, settled in Spain. The sons of Miled, to avenge a relative's murder, resolved to invade Erin. Under the leadership of Heber, Heremon, and Amergin, and accompanied by Scota, a vast army in many ships invaded Ireland. No resistance was offered at first. The Milesians arrived at Tara, and there met the three kings and queens of the Tuatha-de-Danann. The latter complained of being taken by surprise, and asked the Milesians

to embark again on board their ships and allow
them to have a chance of opposing their landing.
The Milesians assented, entered their ships, and
retired for " nine waves " on the sea.   On facing
about again no Ireland was to be seen !   The Tuatha
by their sorcery had made the island as small as a
pig's back, and the Milesians could therefore not
see it.   In addition to this they raised a violent
storm on the sea, with clouds and darkness that
could be felt.   Many Milesian ships were lost, and
the danger was brought to an end only when Amergin,
who was also a Druid, pronounced a Druidic prayer,
or oration, evidently addressed to the Tuatha Dé,
and the storm ceased.   They then landed peaceably ;
but they did not get the island without a few battles
of a very hazy sort indeed.   It probably at first
was intended to be shown that the Tuatha allowed
them to land, and themselves retired to the Land of
Promise—the country of the *Side*—where they still
took an interest in mortal affairs, and often afterwards appeared in Irish history and tales.   The
Milesians, or Gadelians or Gaels, are a purely mortal
race ; they were, in fact, the dominant race of Ireland in historic times.   Their history and full
genealogies from some thirteen hundred years before
Christ till the introduction of Christianity, are gravely
told in the Annals of the Four Masters and Keating's
Ireland ; every king has his pedigree given, and
many are the details that are recorded of their doings
in war and in peace, in society, and in the chase,

in law, and in the care and seizure of land and of cattle. Mythic persons constantly flit across the page ; the demigods become mere mortal chiefs, and the " last reflections " of the sun-god appear in the features of Cuchulainn and Finn.

There are many interpretations put upon the history that we have just summarily given. Naturally enough, ethnological theories form the greater part of such explanations. The leading invasions of the Firbolgs, Fomorians, Tuatha-de-Dannan and Milesians, are made use of to refute or support some favourite theory about the various races that go to compose the Irish nation. Two hundred years ago an Irish genealogist, of the name of Dubaltach MacFirbisigh, advanced the theory, doubtless supported by tradition, that "' every one who is white-skinned, brown-haired, bountiful in the bestowal on the bards of jewels, wealth, and rings, not afraid of battle or combat, is of the Clanna-Miled (the Milesians) ; every one who is fair-haired, big, vindictive, skilled in music, druidry, and magic, all these are of the Tuatha-de-Danann ; while the black-haired, loud-tongued, mischievous, tale-bearing, inhospitable churls, the disturbers of assemblies, who love not music and entertainment, these are of the Feru-bolg and the other conquered peoples." Skene, in modern times, gives this theory of Mac-Firbisigh in our modern terms : the Firbolgs belong to the Iberian or Neolithic and pre-Celtic tribes ; the Celts themselves are divided into Gaels and

Britons ; the Gaelic branch is again subdivided into (1) a fair-skinned, large-limbed, and red-haired race—the Picts of Caledonia and the Tuatha-de-Danann of Ireland ; and (2), a fair-skinned, brown-haired race, " of a less Germanic type," represented in Ireland by the Milesians, and in Scotland by the band of invading Scots. We have already presented the best modern scientific views on the ethnology of these islands ; there would appear to have been three races—(1), A primitive, small, dark, long-headed race, of the Basque type in language and Iberian in physique ; (2), a fair, tall, rough-featured, round-headed, and rough-limbed race, also pre-Celtic, which we called the Finnish ; and (3), the Celts, fair, straight-featured, long-headed and tall, and belonging to the Aryan family. We might equate the Firbolgs with the dark Iberian race ; the Tuatha-de-Danann with the Finnish race ; and the Milesians with the Celts. The legendary and traditional account can easily be fitted into the present scientific view of the subject. But, after all, the truth of such a theory must be gravely doubted ; even its agreement with proper scientific methods in such case must be questioned. We may grant that the strong contrast between a small dark race and a tall fair race might give rise to a myth like that of the Firbolgs and Tuatha-de-Dananns. But in Wales, where the contrast is even stronger, no such myth exists. Again the Milesians were really fair-haired and not brown-haired ; the heroes of Ulster are all fair or yellow-haired, and so are the Feni. It is best, therefore, to adopt a purely mythological explanation of the matter. Despite its pseudo-historical character, the whole history of the invasions of the Firbolg, De-Dananns, and Fomorians appears to be a Gaelic counterpart of what we see in Greek mythology, the war of the rough and untamed powers of earth, sea, and fire, against the orderly cosmos of the Olympians ; the war, in short, of the giants and Titans against Zeus and his brothers. The Firbolgs may be, therefore, looked upon as the earth-powers ; too much stress need not be laid on the fact that they and their brethren, the Fir-Domnans, were wont to dig the soil, make pits, and carry earth in bags to make flowery plains of bare rocks ; but it should be noticed that they always meet the Tuatha-de-Danann as natives of the soil repelling invaders. The gods of the soil often belong to a pre-Aryan people, while the greater gods, the Olympians and the Tuatha-de-Danann, are intrusive, the divinities of the new-comers into the land, the patrons of warriors and sea-faring men. Behind these last there often stand deities of older birth, those who had been worshipped in ancient days by the simple and settled folk of the land. Such were Pan or Hermes of Arcadia, Dionysus of Thrace, and Demeter and Dione. The Firbolgs may, therefore, be looked on as either the homely gods of preceding tribes of the non-Aryan races, or as answering to the giants and Titans of kindred Aryan races. " The King of the Feru-Bolg," says Mr. Fitzgerald, " Eothaile—whom we shall find reason to suspect to be a fire-giant—fled from the field when the day was lost, ' in search of water to allay his burning thirst,' and by the water of the sea he fell on Traigh-Eothaile, ' Eothaile's Strand,' in Sligo. His great cairn, still standing, on this strand was one of the wonders of Ireland, and though not apparently elevated, *the water could never cover it*." If we turn to the Fomorians, we shall find quite as easy an explanation. The meaning of the word is " Sea-rover ; " it has always been derived from the words " fo," under, and " muir," sea, and the meaning usually attached to the combination has been " those that rove on the sea." The Fomorians are, therefore, sea-powers : the rough, chaotic power of the Atlantic Ocean. They meet the Tuatha-de-Dannan in the extreme West of Ireland, on the last day of summer, that is, November eve : the fierce ocean powers meet the orderly heaven and air gods on the Atlantic borders when winter is coming on, and the latter do not allow the former to overwhelm the country. Balor of the Evil Eye, whose glance can turn his opponents into stone, and who, in some forms of the legend, is represented as having only one eye, is very suggestive of Polyphemus, the giant son of the Grecian ocean god. To this we may compare the Gaelic tale of the Muireartach, where the Atlantic Sea is represented as a " toothy carlin," with an eye in the middle of her forehead. The Tuatha-de-Dananns will, therefore, be simply the gods that beneficially direct the powers of sky, air, sea, and earth ; they will correspond exactly to Zeus, Poseidon, Pluto, and the rest of the Grecian god-world, who benignly rule over the heavens, the sea, and the shades. The Milesians will accordingly be merely the main body of the Gaelic people, whose gods the Tuatha-de-Danann are. Why there is no more open acknowledgment of the Tuatha-de-Danann as the pagan gods of the Gael may easily be accounted for. The accounts we have are long posterior to the introduction of Christianity ; and it was a principle of the early Christian Church to assimilate to itself, following the true Roman fashion, all native religions. The native gods were made saints (especially the female divinities, such as Brigit), fairies, demons, and kings. Christianity was about five hundred years established before we have any native record of events ; the further back we go the nearer do the Tuatha-Dé come to be gods. Even in the 8th century an Irish monk could still invoke Goibniu and Diancccht, the Tuatha gods answering to Vulcan and Aesculapius, for relief from, and protection against, pain.

GODS OF THE GAELS.

Whatever interpretation we give to the Ferubolg and the Fomorians, there can be little question

as to the fact that the Tuatha-De-Danann are the
Gaelic gods. The Irish historians, as we saw, represent them as kings with subjects, but even they
find it difficult to hide the fact that some of these
kings and queens afterwards appear on the scene
of history in a super-natural fashion. The myths
and tales, however, make no scruple to tell us that
the Tuatha-De-Danann still live in Fairyland, and
often take part in human affairs. In a very ancient
tract which records a dialogue between St. Patrick
and Caoilte Mac Ronain, they are spoken of as
" sprites or fairies, with corporeal and material
forms, but imbued with immortality." Their skill
in magic, shown in their manipulation of storms,
clouds, and darkness. is insisted on in all the myths,
and is a source of trouble to the historians and
annalists, who regard them as mere mortals. " They
were called gods," says Keating, " from the wonder-
fulness of their deeds of sorcery." To them is first
applied the term *Side*, which in modern Gaelic
means " fairy," but which in the case of the Tuatha-
De-Danann has a much wider signification, for it
implies a sort of god-like existence in the " Land of
Promise." The Book of Armagh calls the *Side*
" deos terrenos," earthly gods, whom, we are told
in Fiacc's hymn, when Patrick came, the peoples
adored—" tuatha adortais *Side*." *Sid* was a term
applied to the green knolls where some of these
deified mortals were supposed to dwell : the word
appears in the modern Gaelic *sith* and *sithean*, a

mound or rather a fairy mound. The Tuatha-De-
Danann were also called " Aes Side," *aes* being here
used in the sense of " race " and not of " age." We
may remark that the Norse gods were also known
as the Aes or Aesir, one of the many remarkable
coincidences in words and in actions between the
Irish gods and the deities of Asgard.

In attempting to reconstruct the Gaelic god-world
from the almost hopeless ruins in which piety and
time have laid it, we must not merely remember
the Aryan character of it, but also Cæsar's brief
account of the Gaulish Olympus. There can be
little doubt but that the Gaelic and Gaulish Olympi
were similar in outline, and probably also in details.
We shall, therefore, expect Mercury to be the most
important of the Gaelic deities, while Apollo, Mars,
Jupiter, and Minerva take rank after him. These
deities and others, as was pointed out, represent
the personified powers of nature—the wind, the
sun, the storm, the sky, and the moon. Not only
are these elements personified as deities and so
worshipped, but we also find the elements in their
impersonified state, as it were, invoked for aid and
for good faith. The classical examples of this are
extremely numerous. One instance will suffice :
In Virgil, Æneas and Latinus are represented as
swearing by the sun, the earth, the sea, the stars,
by the Almighty Father and his Spouse, by Mars
and Janus, by the spring and rivers, the ether and the
deities of the sea. The first instance of such an

oath in Irish history is when Breas, the Fomorian, swore by " the sun and the moon, by the sea and the land, and by all the elements, to fulfil the engagement " which Luga imposed on him. Vows to the heavens and the earth, to day and night, to the rain, the dew and the wind, are exceedingly common, appearing even in historic times both in Ireland and Scotland ; among the Picts and Scots in the 4th century, in Ireland in the 5th, as when Loegaire was made to swear by the elements that he would never again demand the cow-tribute, and with M'Conglinne in the 8th century. It is said that Loegaire forgot his oath, and thus met with an evil end, for " it was the sun and the wind that wrought his death, because he had violated their sanctity ; " so say the Four Masters, good Christians though they were ! The divine elements are known in Gaelic as *duli*, and one of the oldest and most favourite epithets of the Deity is " rig na n-dul," the King of the Elements, to which may be compared " Dia nan dul " of the Gaelic Psalms : the word for Creator in old Gaelic is *Dulem*, the genitive of which is *Duleman*.

Our description of the Gaelic gods will naturally begin with the Jupiter of the Gaels. This honour belongs most probably to the Dagda, " in Dagda mor," " the great good one " (?) as Mr. Fitzgerald explains his name. Some interpret the name as the " good fire." In any case, *dag* signifies " good," appearing in modern Gaelic as *deagh*, but what *da* means is yet undecided. Though the Dagda is very often mentioned, yet little information is given about him. He was one of the leaders of the Tuatha-De-Danann from Scythia to Ireland, and he brought with him from " Murias " a magical cauldron capable of satisfying the hunger of everyone. He is the most renowned of all the Tuatha for his skill in Druidism. With Luga he makes and carries out al the arrangements of the second battle of Moytura, in which, however, he was wounded with a poisoned weapon by the amazon queen Cethlenn. The venom of that wound caused his death 120 years later. For eighty years previous to his death, he ruled the Tuatha as king. There is little in these meagre details to help us to a true notion of the character of the Dagda. It is in the epithets attached to his name, and the incidental references to him, scattered through many tales, that we can hope to understand his position among the gods. He is called Eochaidh Ollathair, that is, Chevalier All-father, and, further, Ruadrofhessa, " the red one of all knowledge." The epithet " Ollathair "—All-father—puts him on a level with Jupiter, Zeus, and Odin ; he is the father of gods and men, king of heaven and earth. Zeus, we know, is the sky-god, the beneficent power of light and life, who regulates the atmosphere and its phenomena—notably, the thunder—for the good of men : Odin is, however, a wind-god more than a sky-god, answering rather to the Roman Mercury and the Greek Hermes than to Jove and Zeus. Is

the Dagda a wind-god or a light-god or a fire-god ?
Mr. Fitzgerald classes him with Odin as a sky- and
wind-god, and appeals to the epithet " Eochaid "
—horseman—as confirmation ; for horseman and
huntsman are nearly allied, and seem rather to
belong to the wind deity, as in the case of Odin
they do so apply. Mr. Elton makes the Dagda
a spirit of heat who ruled all fires in earth and heaven,
for he interprets the name after O'Donovan as signifying " the great good fire." The view which we
will adopt on the matter differs from both the foregoing. The Dagda represents rather the sky-god,
exactly the Roman Jove. He is the All-father ;
he is the Red-one—the sky in certain states being so,
just as at other times he is said to be " greyer than
the grey mist "—who is all-wise ; he is the Dagda,
the good-father or good-one, the deus optimus
maximus, the benign providence, who arranges,
provides, and superintends everything. His
cauldron is interpreted by some as the canopy of
heaven ; like the thunder-god, Thor, he possessed a
hand-stone which returned of itself to the place
from which it was thrown, just as Thor's hammer—
the thunder-bolt—did.

The most important deity in the Gaelic pantheon
must have been Mercury : which of the Tuatha-De-
Danann was he ? The honour of being the god
most worshipped by the Gael must fall to Manannan,
the son of Lir, whose attributes we have already
discussed. Manannan is always a deity ; he is never

a mortal hero like the others. We represented him as god of sea and wind, as opposed to Mr. Elton's view, who made him a sun-god. There is little doubt but Manannan is a wind-god : he possesses all the prominent requisites of such a deity. He is the owner of the wonderful steed, Enbarr, of the flowing mane, who is swift as the cold clear wind of spring ; his also is the sword, from whose wound there was no recovery ; and he possessed the curious mantle that will cause people never to meet again. The three characteristic possessions of Odin are his sword, his mantle, and his horse Sleipnir. The sword is the lightning ; the mantle is the air and clouds, and the grey horse Sleipnir is the rushing grey cloud driven by the wind. Odin is, as already said, mostly a wind-god ; so, too, is Manannan. Both deities, however, usurped features belonging to more departmental gods, in proportion as they took the first place in the worship of the people. Manannan also possessed the wonderful canoe which could hold any number of people, suiting its size to them, and which obeyed the will of those it bore, and swept over the ocean as fast as the March wind. He, too, instituted the " Feast of Age," known as the feast of Gobnenn the smith. Whoever was present at it, and partook of the food and drink, was free ever after from sickness, decay, and old age. The Land of Promise is often identified with *Inis-Mhanann*, or Isle of Man, which was ruled over by Manannan, but his connection with the land of

promise is rather more like that of Mercury with the
land of shades ; he would appear to have been the
psychopomp—the conductor of the shades of men to
the happy Isles of the West. He was, as we saw,
god of merchandise and also god of arts, for he
is represented as teaching Diarmat in all the arts
when he was with him in Fairyland. Why the Celts
and Teutons made the wind deity their chief god is
fairly clear. The atmospheric conditions of Western
and Northern Europe make the wind and storm
powers of comparatively more importance than they
are in sunnier lands, where the gods of light on the
other hand are supreme. Manannan is further
very properly denominated the " son of Lir," the
son of the sea, for sure enough where else does the
wind come from in these islands of ours but from the
sea ?

There is little trouble in settling the identity of
the Gaelic Apollo. This is Luga Lamfada, surnamed
the Ildana ; Luga of the Long Arms, the many-
arted one. He appears with a stately band of
warriors on white steeds, " a young champion, tall
and comely, with a countenance as bright and glorious
as the setting sun." But more definite still is the
reference to his *sunlike* countenance ; in another
place the Fomorian champion, Breas, is made to say
in reference to the approach of Luga from the
west : "A wonderful thing has come to pass to-day ;
for the sun, it seems to me, has risen in the west."
" It would be better that it were so," said the

Druids. "The light you see is the brightness of the face and the flashing of the weapons of Luga of the Long Arms, our deadly enemy." He also possessed the swiftness and keenness of the ocean-wind-god Manannan, for we are told that he rode Manannan's mare Enbarr of the flowing mane, that is, the driving wind ; his coat of mail—the clouds ; and he is further represented as having Manannan's sword, the lightning flash. But this last is doubtful, for two of the precious jewels that the Tuatha-De-Danann took from the east are Luga's sword and his spear "Gae Buaifneach," tempered in the poisoned blood of adders. These weapons are merely the flashing rays of the sun, just as Luga's helmet, Cannbarr, glittered with dazzling brightness, with two precious stones set in it, one in front and one behind. Whenever he took off the helmet, we are told that his " face shone like the sun on a dry summer day." His deeds are also " sunlike " in their character. He first frees the Tuatha from the hated tribute which was imposed on them after a temporary success on the part of the Fomorians. We are told that he put a Druidical spell on the plundered cattle, and sent all the milch cows home to their owners, leaving the dry cows to cumber his enemies. The cows of the sun-god are famous in all mythologies ; they are the clouds of heaven that bring rain and moisture to men, when shone upon by the rays of the sun. Luga's greatest feat is the overthrow of the Fomorians at Moytura. For years he had been preparing for this great fight. He summoned all the artists and artificers of renown and got arms in readiness. He himself lent his help to each tradesman, for he was a skilled carpenter, mason, smith, harper, druid, physician, cup-bearer, and goldsmith, " one who embodied in himself all these arts and professions," as he described himself on one occasion. When the sons of Turenn slew his father, he made them procure for him as " eric " or fine, several weapons of importance and several salves, with a view to using them in the great struggle against the stormy ocean powers. Such were the apples of Hisberna, which could cure any sickness and would return to the owner even when thrown away ; the pig's skin whose touch made whole ; the spear—" the slaughterer "—whose fiery, blazing head was always kept in the water; the steeds and chariot of Dobar—the steeds which travel with equal ease on land and sea ; the pigs of Asal—" whosoever eats a part of them shall not suffer from ill health "—even when killed to-day they are alive to-morrow ; and the hound-whelp Failinis, that shines like the sun on summer day—before him every wild beast falls to earth powerless. In the battle of Moytura, he killed Balor of the Evil Eye. That worthy had already turned Nuada of the Silver Hand into stone, and many more De-Danann, and just as he was opening it on Luga, the latter flung a " sling stone " at it, which passed through it and Balor's brain. Now

Balor was his grandfather, and it had been foretold that he should be slain by his grandson. In view of this he kept his only child, a daughter, Aethlenn, secluded in a tower, where man and the idea of " man " were to be strictly excluded. But in vain She became the wife of Cian, the son of Diancecht, the physician, and Luga was the offspring. We must note his connection with the god of healing ; that god is his grandfather. In Greek mythology, Aesculapius is the son of Apollo. The name Luga, too, is suggestive ; it is doubtless from the root *luc*, to shine, and it is interesting to observe that the Norse fire-god, also master of many arts, though evil arts, is called Loki. The epithet *Lamfada*, long arms, reminds us of the far-darter Apollo, and refers to the long-shooting rays of the sun—a most appropriate epithet.

Cormac informs us in his Glossary that Neith was the god of battle among the pagan Gael, and that Nemon was his wife, information which is repeated in other and later manuscripts with some variations and additions. We are vouchsafed no further information as to Neith's character or actions ; only he appears in some of the inevitable pedigrees, and we are told that Neit, son of Indu, and his two wives, Badb and Nemain, were slain at Ailech by " Neptur (!) of the Fomorians." With Nemain may be compared the British war goddess Nemetona, whose name appears on an inscription along with that of Mars Lucetius. There would appear to have

been more than one war goddess; the names Badb,
Nemain, Macha, and Morrigan, constantly recur as
those of war deities and demons. Badb signifies
a scald-crow, and may be the generic name of the
war goddess rather than a proper name. The crow
and the raven are constantly connected in the
Northern Mythologies with battle-deities. " How
is it with you, Ravens ? " says the Norse " Raven-
song," " whence are you come with gory beak at the
dawning of the day. There is flesh cleaving to
your talons, and a scent of carrion comes from your
mouth. You lodged last night I ween near where
ye knew the corses were lying." The greedy hawks
of Odin scent the slain from afar. The ravens
also protect and assist heroes, both in Irish and
Norse myth. It was a lucky sign if a raven followed
a warrior. Of Macha, the third goddess mentioned,
little need be said ; she appears afterwards as a
queen of Ireland, under the title of Macha Mongruad,
or Macha Red-Mane. The goddess Morrigan was
also a war deity to all appearance. The name
signifies " great queen," and may be, like Badb, a
generic name. She is represented as first resisting
and afterwards assisting the hero Cuchulainn,
appearing to him in various forms. O'Curry makes
her the wife of the Dagda, and she is often equated
with the goddess Ana. The name is doubtless the
same as that of Morgan le Fay, the fairy queen
and Arthur's sister. It may be remarked that
Morgan le Fay is also wife of Urian Rheged, who

and his son Owen, with the army of ravens, are clearly war deities.

The goddess Ana or Aine (gen. Anann) has been called the queen of heaven, and connected with the worship of the moon. Cormac describes her as " mater deorum Hibernensium "—mother of the Irish gods. " Well she used to nourish the gods," he adds, and in another place he says, " As Ana was mother of the gods, so Buanann was mother of the Fiann (heroes)." Camden found in his time survival of moon-worship. " When they see the moon first after the change," he says, " commonly they bow the knee and say the Lord's Prayer, and then, with a loud voice, they speak to the moon, thus—' Leave us whole and sound as thou hast found us." ' Keating gives the name of this goddess as Danann, and explains the Tuatha-De-Danann as the worshippers of the gods of Danann, the gods of Danann being, according to him, Brian, Iucharba, and Iuchar. These three gods are known on other myths as the " children of Turenn," slain, as Keating himself says, by Luga Lamfada. The goddess Buanann, mentioned in connection with Ana or Anann, appears in the story of the great Druid Mogh Ruith as his patron, to whose *Sid* he fares to consult her in his difficulties.

Minerva is the fifth and last deity mentioned by Cæsar as worshipped by the Gauls—their goddess of arts and industry. A passage in Solinus, and another in Giraldus Cambrensis, enable us to decide,

with absolute certainty, what goddess answered
among the Gaels to the position of Minerva. Solinus
(first century A.D.) says that in Britain, Minerva
presides over the hot springs, and that in her temple
there flamed a perpetual fire, which never whitened
into ashes, but hardened into a strong mass.
Giraldus (12th century A.D.) informs us that at the
shrine of St. Brigit at Kildare, the fire is never
allowed to go out, and though such heaps of wood
have been consumed since the time of the Virgin,
yet there has been no accumulation of ashes. " Each
of her nineteen nuns has the care of the fire for a
single night in turn, and on the evening before the
twentieth night, the last nun, having heaped wood
upon the fire, says, ' Brigit, take charge of your own
fire, for this night belongs to you.' She then leaves
the fire, and in the morning it is found that the
fire has not gone out, and that the usual quantity
of fuel has been used." This sacred fire was kept
burning continually for centuries, and was finally
extinguished, only with the extinction of the monas-
teries by Henry VIII. Brigit, therefore, is the Gaelic
Minerva. She is goddess of the household fire ;
her position is that of the hearth goddess Vesta,
as much as that of Minerva, for evidently she is
primarily a fire-goddess. Her name is probably
from the same root as the English *bright*, Gaelic
breo. The British goddess, Brigantia, is doubtless
the same as the Irish Brigit. Mr. Whitley Stokes
picks out the following instances in proof of her

character as a fire-goddess ; she was born at sunrise ; her breath revives the dead ; a house in which she stays flames up to heaven ; she is fed with the milk of a white red-eared cow ; a fiery pillar rises from her head, and she remains a virgin like the Roman goddess, Vesta, and her virgins—Vesta, whom Ovid tells us to consider " nothing else than the living flame, which can produce no bodies." Cormac calls her the daughter of the Dagda. " This Brigit," he says, " is a poetess, a goddess whom poets worshipped. Her sisters were Brigit, woman of healing ; Brigit, woman of smith work ; that is, goddesses ; these are the three daughters of the Dagda." Doubtless these three daughters, thus distinguished by Cormac, are one and the same person. Brigit, therefore, was goddess of fire, the hearth and the home.

The rest of the Gaelic pantheon may be dismissed in a few sentences. Angus Mac-ind-oc, " the only choice one, son of Youth or Perfection," has been well called the Eros—the Cupid—of the Gael. " He was represented with a harp, and attended by bright birds, his own transformed kisses, at whose singing love arose in the hearts of youths and maidens." He is the son of the Dagda, and he lives at the Brugh of the Boyne ; in one weird tale he is represented as the son of the Boyne. He is the patron god of Diarmat, whom he helps in escaping from the wrath of Finn, when Diarmat eloped with Grainne. The River Boyne is also connected with the ocean-god

Nuada ; it was called the wrist of Nuada's wife. The literary deity was Ogma, brother of the Dagda, surnamed "Sun-face ; " he invented the alphabet known as the Ogam alphabet, and, as was pointed out already, he is mentioned by Lucian as the Gaulish god of eloquence. Three artisan gods are mentioned : Goibniu, the smith, invoked in the St Gall Incantations of the 8th century ; Creidne Cerd, the goldsmith, and Luchtine, the carpenter. These three made the Tuatha arms ; when the smith finished a spear-head, he threw it from his tongs towards the door-post, in which it stuck by the point ; the carpenter had the handle ready, and threw it accurately into the socket ; and Creidne Cerd pitched the nails from his tongs into the holes in the socket of the spear. Thus was the spear finished in less time than we can describe the process. Diancecht was the physician of the gods ; at Moytura battle he prepared a medical bath, into which he plunged the wounded, and they instantly came out whole again, and returned to the fight. The three De-Danann queens, Eire, Fodhla, and Banbha, gave their names to Ireland, but the first is the one which is usually recognised. It may be observed that these names and those of some others of the gods are scattered widely over the topography both of Ireland and Scotland. In the latter country we meet with Eire, and its genitive Erenn in river and district names ; Fodla forms part of Athole, Ath-Fodhla, probably ; Banba appears in Banff ;

Angus the Beautiful gave his name to Angus;
Manannan's name appears in the Isle of Man, and as
the old name of the district at the mouth of the Forth,
still seen in Clack-Mannan.

THE CELTIC ELYSIUM.

All the Aryan nations originally believed in the
existence, after death, of the human soul. This
belief had its root in the " animism " of a more
barbaric period of their existence, and held its place
in the remnants of ancestral worship we meet with in
Rome and Greece, and in the many myths bearing
on the land of shades. Evidently, too, the pre-
Aryan tribes of Europe were strong believers in the
future existence of man's second self, his soul. Their
barrows, dolmens, and stone-circles point distinctly
to their reverence for the dead, and their belief in
their continued existence in another sphere of
nature, from which they visited, helped and ad-
monished their living representatives. Ancestor
worship clearly was their main creed. Hence the
vividness of the belief of the early Northern Aryans—
Celts and Teutons—in future existence, and their
clinging to ancestor worship so long, may arise
from their mingling with a people who was in that
stage of belief; whereas at the dawn of our era,
in Greece and Rome, the whole doctrine of a future
state belonged to the region of languid half-belief.
The aristocracy and the philosophers entirely dis-

believed it. Cæsar, as supreme pontiff of Rome, declared, in his place in the senate, his utter disbelief in another life, and the stern Cato but mildly replied that their ancestors, men, perhaps, as wise as Cæsar, believed that the guilty, after death, were sent to noisome abodes, full of all horrors and terrors. But the classical belief, even at its best—in the poems of Homer—gives but a poor, shadowy, comfortless existence to the spirits of the dead. They lived in Hades, a country which comprised various districts of woe, and of bliss such as it was. The ghost of Achilles says to Ulysses :—" Rather would I live on earth as a poor man's hireling, than reign among all the dead." The gods lived on the heights of Olympus, aloft in heaven, and far apart from the hated abode of the dead, which lay under the earth and ocean. Mortals were all consigned to the grisly realm of Pluto ; even the demi-god Hercules, though living in Olympus, had his ghostly mortal counterpart in Hades. Among the Romans, ancestor worship had a stronger force than in Greece ; their feast of the dead was duly celebrated in the latter half of February, when chaplets were laid on their tombs, and fruit, salt, corn soaked in wine, and violets, were the least costly offerings presented to them. The deification of the Emperors was merely a further development of this ancestor worship. The remembrance of the festival of the dead is still kept up in the Roman calendar as the feast of All Souls. The Celts of Brittany preserve still the remembrance of the ancestor worship on this day ; they put cakes and sweet meats on the graves, and at night make up the fire and leave the fragments of the supper on the table, for the souls of the dead of the family who will come to visit their home.

The Celts would appear to have had a much more vivid belief in future existence than either the Greeks or the Romans. We may pass over the Druidic doctrine of transmigration ; it was doubtless not the popular view of future life. We know as much from some side references in one or two classical writers. So realistic was the Celtic belief in existence after death that money loans were granted on the understanding that they were to be repaid beyond the grave. Valerius Maximus laughs at the Gauls for " lending money which should be paid the creditor in the other world, for they believed that the soul was immortal." Mela tells us one of the Druidic doctrines that was publicly preached and nationally believed in, namely, that the soul was eternal and that there was another life in the land of shades. " Accordingly," he adds, " they burn and bury along with the dead whatever was once useful to them when alive. Business accounts and debt claims used to be transferred to the next world, and some even willingly cast themselves on the funeral piles of their relatives under the impression that they would live with them hereafter." Diodorus Siculus informs us that at the funeral of their dead some threw letters addressed to their defunct relatives on the funeral pyre, under the belief that the dead would read them. This intense belief in the reality of future existence must have removed the Celtic other-world from the unreal and shadowy Hades of Greece and Rome. What the exact character of this other world was among the Gauls we cannot well say ; but the later legends in France, Wales, and Ireland go to prove that it partook of the nature of an Earthly Paradise, situated in some happy isle of the West. The pseudo-Plutarch introduces a grammarian Demetrius as returned from Britain, and saying " that there are many desert islands scattered round Britain, some of which have the names of being the islands of genii and heroes. The island which lay nearest the desert isles had but few inhabitants, and these were esteemed by the Britons sacred and inviolable. Very soon after his arrival there was great turbulence in the air and portentous storms. The islanders said when these ceased that some one of the superior genii had departed, whose extinction excited the winds and storms. And there was one island where Saturn was kept by Briareus in a deep sleep, attended by many genii as his companions." The poet Claudian evidently records a Gaulish belief in the Island of Souls in the lines :—

> " Est locus extremum pandit quâ Gallia litus,
> Oceani praetentus aquis, ubi fertur Ulixes
> Sanguine libato populum movisse silentem.
> Illic umbrarum tenui stridore volantum
> Felebilis auditur questus. Simulacra coloni
> Pallida defunctasque vident migrare figuras."

Beyond the westermost point of the Gallic shore,
he says, is the place where Ulysses summoned the
shades (as Homer has it). There are heard the
tearful cries of fleeting ghosts ; the natives see their
pallid forms and ghostly figures moving on to their
last abode. The traditions of Brittany, with true
Celtic tenacity, still bear traces of this belief ; at
the furthest extremity of that district, where Cape
Raz juts into the Western Sea, lies the Bay of Souls,
where departed spirits sail off across the sea in ghostly
ships to the happy isles. Procopius, in the 6th
century, enables us to understand what the peasants
of Northern Gaul believed in regard to the Happy
Isles, and to Britain in particular. He confuses
Britain with a fabulous island called Brittia, one
half of which is habitable ; but the other half
divided off by a wall, is set apart to be the home of
ghosts. The fishermen on the continent opposite
to Brittia performed the functions of ferrymen for
the dead. " At night they perceive the door to be
shaken, and they hear a certain indistinct voice sum-
moning them to their work. They proceed to the
shore under compulsion of a necessity they cannot
understand. Here they perceive vessels—not their
own—apparently without passengers. Embarking,
they take the oars, and feel as if they had a burden
on board in the shape of unseen passengers, which
sometimes sinks the boat to within a finger-breadth
of the water. They see no one. After rowing for
an hour, they reach Brittia, really a mortal journey

of over twenty-four hours. Arrived at Brittia, they hear the names of their passengers and their dignities called over and answered ; and on the ghosts all landing, they are wafted back to the habitable world."

So far we have discovered among the early Celts an intense conviction in a personal existence in another world, where they " married and gave in marriage," and into which business transactions of this world might be transferred. Its locality was to the west—an island in the land of the setting sun, or possibly a country under the western waves, for the traditions of Brittany, Cornwall, Wales, Ireland, and Scotland continually insist on the existence of such a land. Buried cities are recorded as existing to the westward of every prominent Celtic cape ; that sunken district of Lyonesse which appears in all Brythonic traditions. The very earthly character of the Celtic world of the departed is seen in the surviving remembrances of it still existent, despite all the Church's efforts, in the mythic tales ; an Earthly Paradise it truly was. We do not find much in Welsh myth bearing on the matter ; it is in Irish and Gaelic tales that we have the material for judging of the character of the Celtic Elysium.

WELSH AND GAELIC ELYSIUM.

The Welsh Hades was known as Annwn. It possessed kings, chiefs, and commons, somewhat like those of this world, only vastly superior—" the comeliest and best equipped people ever seen." Pwyll, Prince of Dyved (South-west Wales), while one day out hunting, lost his companions in his eager pursuit of a stag. Hearing a cry of hounds near him, he approached, and saw the stag brought down by other dogs than his own. " Then he looked at the colour of the dogs, staying not to look at the stag, and of all the hounds that he had seen in the world, he had never seen any that were like unto these. For their hair was of a brilliant shining white, and their ears were red ; and as the whiteness of their bodies shone, so did the redness of their ears glisten." He drove them from the stag, and set on it his own dogs. Immediately there came upon him a man dressed all in grey and mounted on a grey horse, and he reviled Pywll for his discourtesy in turning off his hounds. Pwyll offered to make reparation, and his offer was accepted. The stranger said that he was Arawn, King of one-half of Annwn, and he was at war with Havgan, the other King. Pwyll, if he liked, could overthrow Havgan, who was to come exactly a year thereafter against Arawn. Would Pwyll change places with him and meet Havgan ? He would give him his own personal appearance, and assume Pwyll's, and they could govern each other's kingdoms for a year. This was agreed on. Pwyll took the form of Arawn, and came to Annwn. He never saw anything like the beauty of Arawn's city and the appointments of his courts, " which of all the courts on earth was the best supplied with food and drink, and vessels of gold and royal jewels." Suffice it to say that he ruled well during the year, and at the end of it slew Havgan, " at the ford," in single combat, and thus made Arawn undisputed master of Hades. Arawn had, meanwhile, conducted the kingdom of Dyved as it never had been before ; his wisdom and justice were unsurpassable. And these two kings made an eternal bond of friendship with each other, and Pwyll was called " Chief of Annwn " henceforward.

The dogs of Annwn, mentioned in the above tale, are a common feature in mythology. Ossian, on his way to Tir-nan-og, saw a hornless fawn bounding nimbly along the wave-crests pursued by a white hound with red ears. The Wild Huntsman and his dogs of Teutonic myth belong to the same category ; and these dogs of Annwn were similarly said to rush through the air, and evil was the omen. These are, undoubtedly, the wind-dogs of Hermes, the conductor of souls ; the Wild Huntsman is none other than Odin, sweeping up the souls of the dead in his path. Annwn, or the Lower Regions, possess, in the myth, the same characteristics as this world ; only things are on a grander scale there altogether.

The other reference of importance to this Earthly Other-world is in the story of Arthur. Dying on the battle-field of Camlan, he is carried away to heal of his wounds to " the vale of Avilion," which Tennyson, catching the true idea of the Welsh mythic paradise, describes thus : Arthur, dying, speaks to Bedivere ;

> " I am going a long way—
> To the island-valley of Avilion ;
> Where falls not hail, or rain, or any snow,
> Nor ever wind blows loudly ; but it lies
> Deep-meadow'd, happy, fair with orchard lawns
> And bowery hollows crowned with summer sea."

And here Arthur still lives on, destined one day to appear and set free his Cambrians from the hateful yoke of the Saxon.

The myths in Ireland bearing on the existence of a happy western land are very numerous and important. The names given to this land vary, but they have a general reference to happiness, all save the name Tir-fa-tonn, the " Under-wave Land." The names generally met with are Tir Tairngire, " Land of Promise ; " Mag Mell, " Plains of Happiness ; " Tir-nam-beo, " Land of the Living ;' Tir-nan-og, " Land of the Young ; " and O'Breasail, " Breasal's Isle." Whether there is any distinction implied in these names cannot well be said. There would seem to be something of a difference between the Under-wave Land and the Plains of Happiness ; the latter may have rather been the abode of the gods, where Manannan lived with Fann his wife, as the myths have it. Tir-fa-tonn looks rather like the Gaelic Hades, the abode of the dead. The Gaelic version of Diarmat's sojourn there gives strong colour to such a supposition, and the early Middle Age legends in regard to St. Patrick's Purgatory below Lough Dearg—the precursors of Dante and Milton's descriptions—lend great countenance to such a distinction between Tir-fa-tonn and Mag Mell.

The myths may be grouped in three divisions. There are, first, the myths where a mortal is summoned, in an enchanting song, by a fairy being who has fallen in love with the mortal, to a land of beauty and happiness and ever-youthful life ; second, there are myths which tell how a hero has, Ulysses-like, paid a business visit to the other world ; and, thirdly, the accounts of many voyages of discovery in search of the Happy Isles, and the " Traveller's Tales " of the wonders seen. To the first class belong three very remarkable Irish myths : the Courtship of Etain, the story of Condla Cam, and Ossian in Tir-nan-og. The outline of the story is as follows :— There suddenly appears before a kingly company a fairy being who chants, for some particular person in the company loved by the fairy, a song descriptive of the glories and pleasures of the Land of the Ever-young. The person so addressed cannot choose but love the fairy, and go to the wonderful land. In Ossian's case alone have we got an account of the

career of the enchanted one in Tir-nan-og. Niam
of the Golden Hair suddenly presents herself before
the Feni, tells her love for Ossian, and says : " I
place you under obligations which no true heroes
break through—to come with me on my white
steed to Tir-nan-og, the most delightful and renowned
country under the sun. Jewels and gold there are
in abundance, and honey and wine ; the trees bear
fruit and blossoms and green leaves all the year
round. Feasting and music and harmless pastimes
are there each day. You will get a hundred swords,
and robes of richest loom ; a hundred steeds, and
hounds of keenest scent ; numberless herds, and
sheep with fleeces of gold ; a hundred maidens
merry and young, sweeter of mouth than the music
of birds ; a hundred suits of armour, and a sword,
gold-handled, that never missed a stroke. Decline
shall not come on you, nor death, nor decay. These,
and much more that passeth all mention, shall be
yours, and myself as your wife ! " Needless is it
to recount how Ossian went, the wonders he saw
by the way, and the feats he did ; how he found
Tir-nan-og all that it was painted by the Princess
Niam ; how, after three hundred years, he returned
to earth on the white steed, from whose back he was
forbidden to dismount ; how he fell from the steed
when helping the poor weakly mortals that he found
then on earth to raise a huge stone ; and how the
steed rushed off and left him, old and withered and
blind, " among little men."

Visits of the nature of that undertaken by Ulysses,
in Homer, to the Land of Shades, were made by at
least three great champions of the Gael.   These are
Cuchulainn, Cormac Mac Art, and Diarmat O'
Duinn.   We have already referred to Cuchulainn's
helping of Fand, wife of Manannan.   The story
says that, like a wise man, Cuchulainn, when invited
to assist Fand, deserted as she was by her husband,
sent his charioteer Loeg to " prospect " and report
as to the safety of such a journey.   Loeg and his
fairy guide " proceeded until they reached the side
of the island, when they saw the bronze skiff waiting
for them.   They then stepped on to the ship and
landed on the island."   There they found Fand and
her father waiting them.   Professor Rhys very
properly compares this passage to the well-known
boat and ferry of Charon in Classical mythology.
" There can be no mistake," he says, " as to its
[the Isle of the Blest] being the Elysium of the dead,
and that going into it meant nothing less than death
to ordinary mortals ; it was only by special favour
that a mortal might enter it otherwise."   Passing
over Cormac Mac Art's visit to Manannan, and
rescue from death of his wife and two children, we
find a double account of Diarmat's visit to Tir-fa-
tonn—one Irish, one Gaelic.   The Irish one is in
its main features the counterpart of the Welsh
Mabinogion, " The Lady of the Fountain."   Diarmat
fights with the knight of the Fountain, and in
wrestling with him they both fall into the fountain.

Diarmat, arriving at the bottom of it, finds himself
in a most beautiful territory, where he does many
deeds of valour, and helps a distressed prince to a
throne. The Highland tale represents him as shelter-
ing a loathly creature that turns out to be a most
beautiful lady under spells. She is the daughter
of the King of the Land under the Waves. After
presenting Diarmat with a fairy castle, and living
with him some time, she left him for her own country,
a slight quarrel having occurred. He followed her,
crossed on the " Charon " boat, much as already
described in Loeg's case, and arrived at an island,
where down went the boat to a land under the sea !
Here Diarmat found his love, but she was deadly
sick, to be cured only by a drink from a magical
cup in the possession of the King of Wonderland.
This is procured by the help of " the messenger of
the other world," who advised him to have nothing
to do with the King's silver or gold, or even with the
daughter, an advice which Diarmat took, for after
healing her, " he took a dislike to her." Diarmat,
therefore, was allowed to return from the realms of
death.

The " Voyagers' Tales " of Ireland can compare
for sensuous imagination very favourably with any
other country's " Travellers' Tales." Naturally
enough, the tales deal altogether with sea-voyages,
generally to some western islands, and they must
and do contain many reminiscences of the Happy
Isles, where the dead live and the gods reign. De-

spite the monkish garb they at times assume, for
two of the most important are undertaken by monks,
the old heathenism peeps out at every turn. Sometimes we hear of a man living in a happy island
with the souls of all his descendants as birds giving
music around him. Sometimes we get a glimpse
of the earthly paradise, where the travellers saw,
" a great number of people, beautiful and glorious-
looking, wearing rich garments adorned and radiant
all over, feasting joyously and drinking from em-
bossed vessels of red gold. The voyagers also heard
their cheerful festive songs, and they marvelled
greatly, and their hearts were full of gladness at all
the happiness they saw and heard. But they did
not venture to land." They pass occasionally into
the regions of spirits, and are brought into contact
with the living and the dead. The wonders they
meet with often point a moral, for there are punish-
ments for wickedness. On one island was found a
man digging with a spade, the handle of which
was on fire, for on earth he was accustomed to dig
on Sunday. On another island was found a burly
miller feeding his mill with all the perishable things
of which people are " so choice and niggardly in this
world." Islands of lamentation and islands of
laughing are visited ; gorgeous palaces and towns,
both above and below the waves, are seen, and duly
described. The principal voyagers were St. Brendan,
the sons of Ua Corra and Maelduin.

No argument as to the character of the inhabitants of the next world can be drawn from the modern names given to it. Flaithemnas or, Gaelic, Flaith-eamhnas, meant " glory " in its original sense, being derived from the word " Flaithem," a lord, with the abstract termination—*as*. " Innis," an island, forms no part of the word so that the old derivation and its consequent theories—" Island of chiefs "—fall to the ground. In the same way do the many weird speculations upon the place of pain, fail. Uffern, in Welsh, and Ifrinn or Iutharn, in Gaelic, are both borrowed from the Latin word, *Infernum*, much to the misfortune of those Druidic theories that make the Celtic hell an " Isle of the Cold Waves." Both Flaitheamhnas and Ifrinn are Christian ideas, and have no counterpart in the Pagan Mythology of the Celts. Our Celtic myths warrant us to speak but of an earthly Paradise, a home of sensuous ease for the departed soul. The glimpses of places of woe in the " Voyagers' Tales " are too much inspired by Christian thought to render speculation upon the Celtic " prison-house " for the soul possible.

What character of body did the spirits of the dead possess, according to the opinions of the Celts ? The sensuous paradise argues a material body capable of both physical enjoyments and sorrows. The gods, of course, had bodies somewhat analogous to those of men ; these bodies were celestial, but yet quite as substantial as human bodies. The difference was that they were not subject to the trammels

of gravitation and visibility, unless they chose.
Their persons were more beautiful and majestic
than those of men ; a " sublimated " humanity
characterised them. They appeared among mortals
—sometimes all of a sudden in the midst of an as-
sembly ; ate, drank, and acted, like mortals, in every
respect. Sometimes they were seen only by one
person in the company, though heard by all, as in
the story of Condla Cam, whom the fairy enchanted
and abducted. These are, however, the Pagan
gods as seen in Christian myth. Yet we find the
ghosts of departed heroes appearing in much the
same way as the *Side* and Tuatha-De-Danann. The
ghost of Caoilte is met with in one or two myths
representing different times—in St. Patrick's time
and King Mongan's time—and on each occasion he
appears in " his habit as he lived," full of life and
colour, not pale and shadowy. Besides, these
ghosts can appear in the day time, as Caoilte used
to do. The great poem of the Tain Bo Chuailgne
had been lost by the 6th century and it could be
recovered only by raising its composer, Fergus
MacRoy, from the dead. And this the Saints of
Erin were able to accomplish. " Fergus himself,"
we are told, " appeared in a beautiful form, adorned
with brown hair, clad in a green cloak, and wearing
a collared gold-ribbed shirt, a gold-hilted sword,
and sandals of bronze." He was evidently a very
substantial apparition ! St Patrick was also able,
though indirectly, to raise the spirit of the great

Cuchulainn himself, to meet King Loegaire. The famous champion appeared to him one morning splendidly dressed, with his chariot, horses, and charioteer, the same as when alive. All is minutely described : the charioteer, for instance, was a "lƏnk, tall, stooped, freckle-faced man. He had curling reddish hair upon his head. He had a circlet of bronze upon his forehead which kept his hair from his face ; and cups of gold upon his poll behind, into which his hair coiled ; a small winged cape on him, with its buttoning at his elbows ; a goad of red gold in his hand, by which he urged his horses."

The substantial ghosts of dead heroes are in the myths generally classed as *Side*, among whom also the gods were classed. This, of course, arose from a confusion. The *Side*, I take it, were the ghosts of the glorious dead dwelling in their barrows or tumuli (the *sid*). At these barrows, doubtless, they were worshipped in accordance with the customs of ancestor worship. This cannot be proved with satisfaction from the Gaelic myths alone, but if we refer to the belief and rites of the Norse peoples, we shall see plenty evidence of the worship of the dead in their barrows. In the Land nama-bok we read that at one place " there was a harrow (' high place ') made there, and sacrifices began to be performed there, for they believed that *they died unto these hills*." The editors of the lately published work, " Corpus Poeticum Boreale," bring forward quite an array of evidence in proof of the sacredness

of these " houses " and barrows, and the belief
that dead ancestors lived another life there, and took
an interest in the living. " Of the spirit life and the
behaviour of the dead," they say, " there is some
evidence. In the older accounts they are feasting
happily, and busying themselves with the good of
their living kindred, with whom they are still united
in intense sympathy. . . . Of the ritual names
of the worshipped dead, the oldest we know is ' Anse,'
which survived in Iceland into the Middle Ages,
in the sense of guardian spirit or genius of a hill.
' Elf ' is another name used of spirits of the dead—
of divine spirits generally—as the ' Anses ' and the
' Elves ' of Loka-Senna. Later, in Christian times,
it sinks in Scandinavia to mean ' fairy.' . . . .
There were *evil spirits*—spirits of bad men—and even
vampires and the like, such as the dreadful Glam
and unhallowed spirits and monsters." We may
thus argue that the *Side* or *Aes-Side* (compare Anse
or Aesir above) were properly the divine ancestors,
and that the gods, originally in Pagan times quite
distinct from them, were afterwards confused with
the " sidè," as we have them in the myths. But
a still greater confusion overtook these names and
ideas as time and Christianity advanced. The
" sidè " got mixed up with the " elves," the earth
and wood powers, just as they did among the Norse ;
and the modern " sith " is a mixture of tumulus-
dweller and wood-nymph. The gods have almost
entirely left the scene ; only the Lares—the Grua-

gachs and Brownies are left. Of old, among the
Pagan-Gael, there were, doubtless, ghosts somewhat
analagous to those of present superstitions, but they
were clearly those of unhallowed men, as we have
seen in the case of the Norse beliefs. The modern
ghosts follow the analogy of the dwellers in the
Greek Hades, and not of the inhabitants of the
Earthly Paradise of the Gaels, that "·Land of the
Leal " where the sun sinks in the west. They grew
up during the Middle Ages under the shadow of the
Roman Church.

CELTIC WORSHIP AND RITES.

A brief glance at the places and rites of worship
and burial among the ancient Celts will conclude
the religious aspect of their Mythology. The Celts
worshipped in temples and in groves ; both are
frequently referred to in the classical writers. Unfortunately no description of any Celtic temple is
vouchsafed us ; the natural conclusion we must
come to is that they must have been similar, however rude, to the temples of the kindred races of
Greece and Rome. Celtic houses were constructed
of wood : " great houses," says Strabo, " arched,
constructed of planks and wicker, and covered with
a heavy thatched roof." They were circular, high,
and with either a conical or domed roof. This
description applies to the very earliest Celtic buildings, those of Britain and rural Gaul, for the Gauls

of Cæsar's time had towns with walls, streets and
market places, as opposed to the "dunum," the
stockaded hill-top or fortified forest-clearing, of their
insular brethren. The Gaulish temples must, therefore, have been of stone, but the British temples
were most likely constructed, like the houses, of
wood. The earliest Christian churches were also
made of wood, and, for the most part, clearly consisted of the old heathen temples consecrated to
Christian use. "The temples of the Idols in Britain,"
says Pope Gregory (A.D. 601), "ought not to be
destroyed ; but let the idols that are in them be
destroyed ; let holy water be made and sprinkled
in the said temples ; let altars be erected and relics
placed." There are no remains of either Celtic
heathen temples or early Christian churches. The
theory that the so-called "Druid" circles were
Celtic temples is refuted by the two facts that the
Celts were Aryans with Aryan culture, and that they
made use of metal—even iron—tools from the earliest
period we have record of them. The rude stone
circles are evidently not the work of a race well
acquainted with the use of metal. It is quite true
that in religious ceremonies old phases of culture,
whether of dress, instruments, or buildings, survive
in a higher stage of civilisation. Thus the flint
knife of the "stone" age was used on solemn
occasions at the Jewish circumcision, and at the
sacrifices of old Carthage and Rome ; and the gowns
of modern clergymen are the survivals of Middle-Age

dresses. This, however, operates but to a limited
extent ; the Jewish temple, unlike their rude stone
altars, was built of *hewn* stone, made ready before
being brought to the temple, so that " there was
neither hammer nor axe, nor any tool of *iron*, heard
in the house while it was building." In this way
a metal-using people reconciled the old with the
new phase of culture, and we cannot suppose that
the Celts, even if they did use stone circles, which
is most improbable, would not have reconciled them
to their state of culture by dressing and shaping
the stones, as, indeed, the Bronze Age builders of
Stonehenge had begun to do.

Along with temples, the classical writers continually mention " groves " as especial places where
Celtic worship was conducted. A grove was a secret
recess embowered by tall trees, and marked by
votive offerings, insignia of the gods, and an altar
of stone, or some equivalent. The distinguishing
features of a grove were secrecy and sacredness.
Groves are prior in time to temples, and Grimm has
analysed the Teutonic words for " temple " to
signify " wood " or even " grove." He says—
" The earliest seat of heathen worship was in groves,
whether on mountain or in pleasant mead ; there
the first temples were afterwards built, and there
also were the tribunals of the nation." The classical
words for temple—Latin, *templum*, Greek, *temenos*,
both from the root *tem*, to cut, mean, originally, a
" clearing "—a forest clearing, in fact. The Greek

temenos, which may mean a sacred grove, is often used in speaking of Celtic places of worship. The Gaulish word of like signification was *nemeton*, which appears in several place-names in Britain, Gaul, and Asia Minor ; in the latter country the Galatian council of the twelve tetrarchies met at a place called Drynemeton, that is, " oak-grove." In old Irish, the word appears as *nemed*, a chapel, and is the same in root as the Gaelic *neamh*, heaven, and the Latin *nemus*, a grove. Lucan, in the following lines, gives us a vivid description of a Gaulish grove, dwelling on the superstitions and miracles connected with it, and alluding to the worship of the " secretum illud," the abstract existence, which Tacitus says the Germans reverenced, who, here as elsewhere in religion, differed but little from the Celts.

> " A grove, inviolate from length of age,
> With interwoven branches' mazy cage,
> Enclosed a darkened space of earth and air,
> With chilly shades, where sun could enter ne'er.
> There not the rustic gods nor satyrs sport,
> Nor sylvans, gods of groves, with nymphs resort ;
> But barbarous priests, on altars dire, adore
> Their gods, and stain each tree with human gore.
> If miracles of old can be received
> And pious tales of gods can be believed,
> There not the feathered songster builds her nest,
> Nor lonely dens conceal the savage beast ;
> There no tempestuous winds presume to fly,
> Ev'n lightnings glance aloof, obliquely by.
> Nor ever breezes lift or lay the leaves,
> But shivering horror in the branches heaves ;
> The plenteous stream the darkened fountains leaves :
> The images of gods, a mournful band,

Have ne'er been shaped so rude by artist's hand—
Misshapen forms with limbs lopped off forth stand.
The very place, with oaks all hoar and drear,
Inspires the gazer's soul with numbing fear :
'Tis not the deities of wonted form
They worship thus 'mid terrors and alarm,
But gods unknown—it but increases fear
They do not know the gods they so revere.
Oft, as fame tells, the earth in throbs of woe
Is heard to groan from hollow depths below ;
The baleful yew, though dead, has oft been seen,
To rise from earth and spring with dusky green ;
With sparkling flames the trees, unburning shine,
And round their boles prodigious serpents twine.
The pious worshippers approach not near,
But shun their gods and kneel with distant fear ;
The priest himself, when Phœbus, god of light,
Rolling, has reached his full meridian height,
Or night rules all, dreads to approach the place
And shuns the master of the grove to face."

The favourite tree among the Gauls for groves was
the oak ; " the Druids," says Pliny, " choose groves
of oak and conduct no sacrifice without its leaf,"
and he suggests that the name Druid is from the
same root as Greek *Drus*, an oak, a derivation which
is yet the only one worth consideration of the many
suggested. The sacredness of groves and of trees
has not yet died out among the Celts. In Ireland
it is counted especially unlucky to cut down trees
in raths and such early structures. Mr. Kinahan,
in the " Folklore Record " for 1882, says :—A
man, near Kilmaganny, County Kilkenny, came to
me in a great state of mind one morning, as the
previous night some one had cut a thorn tree in a

rath on his land, and some ill-luck must come to
him before the end of the year. I tried to console
him by saying the year [it being October] was nearly
out, so that he would probably live out the charm,
but curiously enough before Christmas he buried a
fine girl of a daughter.

The Celts made use of statues in their worship :
Cæsar mentions that there were very many statues
of Mercury, and other writers, as Lucan, in the lines
quoted above, bear testimony to the same fact.
Before they used images, they were content with
emblems of the gods ; thus we are told by a writer
of the second century that the Celts worshipped
Zeus, and that a tall oak represented his statue,
a reference which again puts the Celts on a level
with the Germans of Tacitus, who had no statues,
and even thought it an impiety to represent celestial
grandeur in human shape.   Some remains of Gaulish
art in statue-making have weathered the ravages
of ages, and of these the statuettes of Mercury and
Taranis are the most numerous and interesting.
Uninfluenced by Roman or Greek art, their statues
were rude and unshapely, as Lucan says :—" Simula-
craque maesta deorum arte carent." Gildas speaks
of the grim-faced idols mouldering in the deserted
temples ; and idols of bronze to the number of
nineteen were dug up at Devizes in 1714. A true
Celtic statue called by its Breton votaries the
" Groah-Goard," and known as the " Venus of
Quinipily," was worshipped in Brittany till the

17th century. It was a huge misshapen figure,
7 feet high, with a large and uncouth body, a flattened
bust, and eyes, nose, and mouth like those of an
Egyptian idol. We meet in Irish history with the
mystical figure of Crom or Crom-Cruaich, King-idol
of Erin, first, in the reign of King Tiernmas (1543
B.C.), who, we are told, died along with three-
fourths of his people whilst they were " ic adrad
Cbroim-Chroich, rig idaill hErenn," and, a second
time, in St Patrick's life, who found at Mag
Slecht (" adoration plain ") in Cavan, Crom-Cruaich,
the chief idol of Erin, covered with gold and
silver, and having twelve other idols about it
covered with brass. The saint caused the earth to
swallow these up as far as their heads, where they
still were, as a sign of the miracle, when the pious
Middle-Age scribe was writing.

The Gaulish altars and also the Gaelic altars were
pillars of stone inscribed with emblems of the sun
and moon, or a beast, bird, or something which
symbolised some force of nature—" dealba nan
dula "—representations of the elements, as Cormac
calls them. Another feature of Celtic groves and
temples consisted of the many votive tablets and
images, with representation of limbs, faces, and
bodily parts, hung up on the walls or suspended
from the trees. These were set up as thank-
offerings for rescue from some sickness or pain in the
part represented, or with a view that relief from
pain might come. The " rag-bush " by the modern

wells, and the crutches and other accessories of infirmities left at holy wells, are a remnant of ancient and analogous beliefs in the deities of the fountains. A more ghastly sight, however, would be presented by the many heads of animals, and, possibly, of men hung up in the groves, like trophies of the chase, but really intended as votive offerings, and rendered, at times, all the ghastlier by having their mouths prized and kept open by sticks of wood. This custom is still kept in remembrance in modern architectural designs.

For Celtic religious rites we have to trust almost entirely, in attempting to discover them, to the superstitions and customs of Christian and modern times. Superstition is the survival, in another phase of culture, of earlier religion and science. At present we shall only deal with some customs and superstitions that appear to bear on Celtic religious ritual, leaving the wider question of quaint customs and superstitions to be dealt with afterwards. The classical writers mention but little of Celtic rites. The human sacrifices attracted most attention : " They sacrifice men," says Diodorus, " striking them at the place above the diaphragm [on the back, Strabo says], and from their fall, the convulsion of the limbs and the flow of the blood, they predict the future." When the Romans put a stop to their human sacrifices, vestiges, however, remained, as Mela says, of the old but abolished savagery, and " just as they refrain from going the

whole length of slaughter, they nevertheless touch
and graze the persons devoted to sacrifice after
bringing them to the altars." An interesting
parallel to this in modern times occurs in the Samoan
islands. There cannibalism has for ages been
unknown, yet the punishment that carries the highest
disgrace among them is to put the delinquent into a
cold oven, an evident survival from the time when
such a person would be roasted and eaten. The
remembrance of these old Celtic human sacrifices
was until lately kept up at the Beltane fires.

The only religious rites of any consequence that
can be pointed to are those connected with the
worship of fire and the changes of the year. It
must not be supposed that the Celts were greater
worshippers of fire, sun, and moon than the other
European nations, and that this worship was distinctive of them. The fire worship was equally
as strong among Teutons, Romans, and Greeks as
among the Celts, and quite as long maintained
into modern times. But Celtic idiosyncracies bring
some features of the worship and practices into
greater prominence. The custom of showing reverence by walking round persons or things, keeping
the right hand towards them, is derived from the
apparent course of the sun, and is known as " deiseil "
(*dextralis*), " right-hand-wise." In India the old
name for the custom is similarly the " right-hand
turn," *dakshiman kri*. The " need-fire "—Gaelic,
teine-eiginn—is a " survival " from a very ancient

phase of culture, and, possibly, from a time when men lived in a warmer climate, and the rubbing of sticks easily produced fire. It is also significant that, in the best preserved form of the custom, the need-fire makers must have no metal about them, a survival which points to the Stone Age. Another general fact in regard to Celtic need-fire was that all the district fires within sight had previously to be extinguished, to be re-lighted only from the pure need-fire. The need-fire was variously produced. In Mull, about 1767, a hill-top was selected, within sight of which all fires were put out, and then the pure fire was produced by *turning a wheel over nine spindles of wood* until the friction caused combustion. Martin in his " Western Isles " thus describes it :—" The *tinegin* they used as an antidote against the plague or murrain in cattle, and it was performed thus—All the fires in the parish were extinguished, and then eighty-one married men, being thought the necessary number for effecting this design, took two great planks of wood, and nine of them were employed by turns, who by their united efforts rubbed one of the planks against the other until the heat thereof produced fire ; and from this fire each family is supplied with new fire, which is no sooner kindled than a pot full of water is quickly set on it, and afterwards sprinkled on the people infected with the plague or upon the cattle that have the murrain." In Caithness the friction was produced by working a horizontal wooden

bar, supplied with levers, in two upright pieces
of wood, into which it was inserted at each end.
In all cases, within Christian historic times, the need-
fire was lighted as a charm against the plague,
whether it attacked men or cattle. Fire has always
been considered the purifier *par excellence*, and
clearly no fire could be so pure as the need-fire,
which was there and then produced for the first time.
But though latterly restricted to being a charm
against the plague, the need-fire shows clear traces
of a higher religious purpose. These fires were
lighted at the great festivals of the solar and lunar
year, and from them all the fires of the neighbourhood,
previously extinguished, were re-lighted. Priests,
we know, presided at these sacred fires, and men and
cattle were passed through them, as Cormac and
others tell us. One of St. Patrick's first struggles
with King Loegaire was over the sacred Beltane (?)
fire. " Fire is kindled by him at that place on Easter
Eve," says a Middle-Irish life of the saint ; " Leogaire
is enraged when he sees the fire. For that was a
prohibition of Tara which the Gael had, and no one
durst kindle a fire in Ireland on that day until it
had been kindled first at Tara at the solemnity.
And the Druids said ' unless that fire be quenched
before this night, he whose fire it is shall have the
kingdom of Ireland for ever.' " But that fire was
not quenched, and the boldness of the missionary,
along with the inevitable miracles, brought Loegaire
and his people to the side of the Saint and Christianity.

The need-fire and the sunwise-turn, " deiseil,"
are but the outward embodiments of the great
worship of fire and light. The discovery how to
make fire at will was a tremendous step in human
progress, and has impressed itself on the oldest
mythologies in the many myths in regard to the
"descent of fire." In India the god is taken down
from his hiding place in heaven and given to man,
and his sign is the wooden fire-drill, *pramantha*.
Prometheus and his history represent the Greek
equivalent myth. The sun was reverenced by
imitation of its course—the " deiseil," though, also
as still on the Continent any day, the Gaels at
Beltane morn worshipped the rising sun by taking
off the caps, and saluting him with " failte "
or hail. For distinctive instances of rites
we must have recourse to the observances
and customs of certain festal days throughout the
year.

The year is a solar period, the unit of which is the
day, but ancient peoples felt the want of an intermediate reckoner of time, and this was found in the
moon and its monthly period. In fact, the moon
was the measurer of time *par excellence*, as the words
for month in English, Latin, Greek, and Gaelic
prove, for they are from the root of " moon." Its
four phases give rise to weeks of seven or eight days,
eight among the Romans ; and the Celts, as well
as the Teutons and Greeks, reckoned their time by
nights, and not by days. Pliny informs us that

the Celtic year and the Celtic months began on the
6th day of the moon. Customs and superstitions
in regard to the moon and its waxing and waning
still survive in connection with the cutting of wood
or turf, the starting of new enterprises or of a
journey, and such like. The lunar time does not
square with the solar time of revolution, and the
ancients were in endless confusion in regard to their
calendars. The Celts corrected lunar by solar
time every thirty years, which Pliny tells us was their
cycle. The month may have been alternately 29
and 30 days, to suit the $29\frac{1}{2}$ days of lunar revolution,
and possibly by having 13 lunar months for eleven
years of the thirty, they managed to make the solar
fit with the lunar time to within a few days. The
year was originally divided into two seasons—
summer and winter, *gam* and *sam*, and then spring
was added, the name of which differs in root in the
two great branches of the Celtic race. The week
is most probably non-Celtic in idea, and also in
names to a very great extent. The Welsh names
of the days of the week are Roman ; the Gaelic
names are mixed, Roman and Christian. Sunday
is Di-domhnuich (dies *dominica*) ; Monday, Di-
luain (dies Lunæ) ; Tuesday, Di-Mairt (dies Martis) ;
Wednesday, Di-ciadaoin (dies primi *jejunii*, " day
of first fast ; " for religious people as Bede tells us,
fasted on Wednesdays as well as Fridays), a purely
church name ; Thursday, Di-ardaoin, or Irish, Dia
dardaoin, " day between two fasts ; " Friday, Di-

h-aoine, " day of fast ; " and Saturday, Di-Sathuirne (dies Saturni).

Fire and Sun worship, and along with these, the worship of the earth-powers, fell on the four great solar periods, the two solstices and the two equinoxes. Lunar time was made to fit these by holding the feasts on the first full moon, or the 14th of the month, after the equinox or solstice. The great winter feast on December 25th, when the sun just turned on its northward course again, was solemnised in honour of the new birth of the " unconquered sun," dies natalis invicti solis, and was held in Rome in honour of the sun-god Mithra, of Persian origin, whose festival was finally established by Aurelian as national and Roman, about A.D. 273. A hundred years later the Christian Church accepted it, doubtfully and reluctantly, as the natal day of Christ, thus entering on a course which it consistently pursued of christianising all pagan rites, festivals, and even temples. The midsummer solstice was therefore dedicated to St John the Baptist, and so on. The Celtic, or rather Gaelic festivals, of a distinctive kind, are three in number ; Bealltuinn (1st May), Lunasduinn (1st August), and Samhuinn (1st November). Why these festivals should be a month later than the solar periods in each case, is doubtful ; but it is clear that these periods suit the climatic changes of the seasons in the North better than the earlier, though truer, solar periods.

The great festival of Beltane occurred on May-day.

Cormac's reference to this pagan festival is the first and most important :—" Belltaine, *i.e.* bil tene, a goodly fire, *i.e.* two fires which Druids used to make through incantations (or with great incantations), and they used to bring the cattle to those fires as a preservative against diseases of each year." Here we have to note that the fire was made by Druidic incantations, which means no more than that it was made by the " tinegin," or need-fire method, and that it was a preservative against disease in cattle. Cormac's derivation has the misfortune of making a wrong division of the syllables of the word, which are beallt-uinn, or belt-ane ; not bel-tane. We must reject any derivation that so divides the word, and hold that the latter part of the word has nothing to do with *teine* fire, but is, probably, the—*n* termination of most words of time. Hence derivations which connect the word with the fire of Baal or Bel are out of place, granting that such a god as Bel is Celtic, and not invented for the occasion. Belinu, is the Celtic Apollo. Mr. Fitzgerald's derivation of Beltane, from bile-tineadh, " fire-tree," is to be rejected on the ground of wrong division of the word, and his instances adduced of the existence in Ireland of usages pointing to a belief in a world-tree of the Norse type appear to be too slight and too little founded on general Celtic, especially Scottish, traditions in regard to the Beltane festival. The world-tree, and consequent may-pole, are not distinctively, if at all, Celtic in this connection. " The first of

May," says M. D'Arbois de Jubainville, " was consecrated to Beltene, one of the names of the god of death, the god who gave and took away life," the root in this case being the pre-historic infinitive *beltiu*, to die. Why the festival of the beginning of the summer, the outburst of nature, and the conquest of the death and winter powers should be sacred, not to the god of life and light, but to his opposite, is a thing which this derivation and theory cannot account for. The November feast might well be one where the loss of the sun-god and victory of the god of death were commemorated, but the first of summer is far from appropriate for this. Both in Welsh and Gaelic myth the victory of the light-gods is indicated on the first of May ; Gwyn fights for Cordelia, and the Tuatha de Danann overcame the Firbolg, the Earth powers, on that day. Grimm hesitatingly hints what appears to be the true derivation :—The Norse sun-god is called Balder, and he suggests that this is connected with Lithuanian *baltas*, " white." The connection of Beltane with these two words is confirmed by the Gaelic saying of "la buidhe Bealltuinn," " yellow May-day," which may be a reminiscence of the primary meaning of Beltane.

We have numerous accounts of the Beltane rites, all pointing to fire and sun worship—phases of purification, sacrifice, and divination. One of the best accounts is given in the Old Statistical Account of the parish of Callander. " Upon the first of

May," it says, " which is called Beltan or Bàl-tein, all the boys in a township or hamlet meet on the moors.   They cut a table in the green sod, of a round figure, by casting a trench in the ground of such circumference as to hold the whole company.   They kindle a fire and dress a repast of eggs and milk in the consistence of a custard.   They knead a cake of oatmeal, which is toasted at the embers against a stone.   After the custard is eaten up, they divide the cake into so many portions, as similar as possible to one another in size and shape, as there are persons in the company.   They daub one of these portions all over with charcoal until it be perfectly black. They put all the bits of the cake into a bonnet. Every one, blindfold, draws out a portion.   He who holds the bonnet is entitled to the last bit.   Whoever draws the black bit, is the devoted person who is to be sacrificed to Baal, whose favour they implore in rendering the year productive of the sustenance of man and beast.   There is little doubt of these inhuman sacrifices having been once offered in this country, as well as in the East, although they now pass from the act of sacrificing, and only compel the *devoted* person to leap three times through the flames ; with which the ceremonies of the festival are closed."   To this sensible account and its inferences, all but the reference to Baal, we agree fully. Most authorities hold, with Cormac, that there were two fires, between which and through which they passed their cattle and even their chil-

dren. Criminals were made to stand between the
two fires, and hence the proverb, in regard to a
person in extreme danger, as the Rev. D. Macqueen
gives it, " He is betwixt two Beltein fires." Pennant
adds some interesting facts : the rites began with
spilling some caudle on the ground by way of libation,
whereupon " everyone takes a cake of oatmeal
upon which are raised nine square knobs, each one
dedicated to some particular being, the supposed
preserver of their flocks and herds, or to some particular animal, the real destroyer of them. Each
person then turns his face to the fire, breaks off a
knob, and flinging it over his shoulders, says, ' This
I give to thee, preserve thou my horses ; this to thee,
preserve thou my sheep,' and so on. After that,
they use the same ceremony to the noxious animals :
' This I give to thee, O fox ! spare thou my lambs :
this to thee, O hooded crow ! this to thee, O eagle.' "
Shaw, the historian of Moray, tells us that the fires
were kindled with a flint; "the Druidic incantations"
of Cormac and the " tinegin " were not used within
the last century at least for lighting the Beltane
fire ; their use seems latterly to have been restricted
to raising the need-fire during cattle plagues.

The midsummer festival, christianised into St.
John's Eve and Day, for the celebration of the
summer solstice, is not a specially Celtic, as it is a
Teutonic feast. The wheels of wood, wrapped round
with straw, set on fire, and sent rolling from a hillock
summit, to end their course in some river or water,

which thus typified the descending course of the sun
onward till next solstice, is represented on Celtic
ground by the occasional use of a wheel for producing the *tinegin*, but more especially by the custom
in some districts of rolling the Beltane bannocks
from the hill summit down its side.   Shaw remarks :
" They made the Deas-sail [at Midsummer] about
their fields of corn with burning torches of wood
in their hands, to obtain a blessing on their corn.
This I have often seen, *more, indeed, in the Lowlands*
than in the Highlands.   On Midsummer Eve, they
kindle fires near their cornfields, and walk round
them with burning torches."   In Cornwall last
century they used to perambulate the villages carrying lighted torches, and in Ireland the Eve of Midsummer was honoured with bonfires *round which
they carried torches.*

The specially Celtic feast or " Feill " was held
some five weeks later, on the 1st August, Lammas
Day.   It is called in Scottish Gaelic " Lunasduinn,"
in Irish " Lunasd," old Irish " Lugnasad," the fair
of Lug.   The legend says that Luga of the Long
Arms, the Tuatha De Danann king, instituted this
fair in honour of his foster-mother Tailtiu, queen
of the Firbolgs.   Hence the place where it was held
was called Tailtiu after her, and is the modern
Teltown.   The fair was held, however, in all the
capitals of ancient Ireland on that day.   Games
and manly sports characterised the assemblies.
Luga, it may be noted, is the sun-god, who thus

institutes the festival, and it is remarkable that at ancient Lyons, in France, called of old Lug-dunum, a festival was held on this very day, which was famous over all Gaul.

Equal to Beltane in importance was the solemnity of Hallowe'en, known in Gaelic as *Samhuinn* or " summerend." Like Beltan it was sacred to the gods of light and of earth ; Ceres, Apollo, and Dis also, must have been the deities whose worship was honoured. The earth goddess was celebrated for the ingathering of the fruits ; Apollo or Belinus and Proserpine were bewailed for their disappearing from earth, and Dis, who was god of death and winter's cold, and who was especially worshipped by the Celts, as Cæsar says, was implored for mercy, and his subjects, the manes of the dead, had special worship directed to them. It was, indeed, a great festival—the festival of fire, fruits, and death. The features that still remain in popular customs in regard to Hallowe'en clearly show its connection with the gods of fire and fate ; bonfires and divination are its characteristics. The Statistical Account, already quoted, says of Hallowe'en :—" On All-Saint's Even they set up bonfires in every village. When the bonfire is consumed, the ashes are carefully collected in the form of a circle. There is a stone put in, near the circumference, for every person of the several families interested in the bonfire, and whatever stone is moved out of its place or injured before next morning, the person represented by that stone is devoted or *fey*, and is supposed not to live twelve months from that day." A somewhat similar custom is recorded by Pennant as existing in North Wales, where every family made a great bonfire in the most conspicuous place near the house, and when the fire was extinguished, every one threw a white stone into the ashes, having first marked it. If next morning any of these stones is found wanting, they have a notion that the person who threw it in will die before next Hallowe'en. We can only refer to the various laughable and serious methods of divination resorted to on Hallowe'en night to read into the future ; our national poet Burns has left us a graphic picture of the night and its ceremonies in " Hallowe'en." It may be remarked that the mystic apple plays an important part in these ceremonies, as it also does in so many Celtic fairy tales. The custom in various parts of keeping a heap of cakes, called *soul-cakes*, to give away to all-comers, and more especially to the poor, clearly commemorates the ancient offering to the dead of food on this night. What was dedicated in Pagan times to the manes of the dead, is in modern times converted into doles of bread to the poor, as Mr. Tylor points out.

Martin records a religious rite of the Lews people that must not be passed over here. " The inhabitants of this island had an ancient custom to sacrifice to a sea-god called Shony, at Hallotide, in the following manner :—The inhabitants round the

island came to the Church of St Malvey,
having each man his provision along with him ;
every family furnished a peck of malt, and this was
brewed into ale ; one of their number was picked
out to wade into the sea up to the middle, and carrying a cup of ale in his hand, standing still in that
posture, cried out with a loud voice, saying, ' Shony,
I give you this cup of ale, hoping that you'll be so
kind as to send us plenty of sea-ware for enriching
our ground for the ensuing year' ; and so threw the
cup of ale into the sea. This was performed in the
night-time. At his return to land they all went
to church, where there was a candle burning upon the
altar ; and then standing silent for some time, one
of them gave a signal, at which the candle was put
out, and immediately all of them went to the fields,
where they fell a-drinking their ale and spent the
remainder of the night in dancing, singing, etc."
This they believed to be a powerful means to procure
a plentiful crop. This superstition is but lately
dead, though the sacrifice had been repressed, for
they proceeded in spring to the end of a long reef
and invoked " Briannuil " to send a strong north
wind to drive plenty sea-ware ashore. There are
other instances of sacrifice within the last two
hundred years in the Highlands. An annual sacrifice on the 25th August to St Mourie in Applecross
and Gairloch troubled the Dingwall Presbytery in
the 17th century. These rites consisted in immo-
lating bulls, pouring of milk on hills as oblations,

visiting ruined chapels and " circulating " them, divining by putting the head into a hole in a stone, and the worshipping of wells and stones. The bulls were sacrificed " in ane heathenish manner " for the recovery of man and beast from disease. A Morayshire farmer some thirty years ago, in the case of a murrain, lighted the need-fire with all due ceremony, then dug a pit and sacrificed an ox to the " unknown " spirit. Sacrifice of cocks for epilepsy has not been infrequent in modern times ; this is done by burying them alive.

Other festival days retain a spice of heathen Celticism about them yet. The last night of the year the fire must not be allowed to go out, and there is a particular dislike at this time to give a neighbour a " kindling " or even light for a pipe, a feeling which in some degree exists at Beltane and Hallowe'en. Candlemas day is known as La Fheill-Brighde, St Brigit's day, who is really the canonised fire-goddess, the Vesta of the heathen Gaels. Some customs in regard to her worship were mentioned already, and Martin relates an interesting custom in the Western Isles on Candlemas, showing St Brigit clearly in the aspect of Vesta, the hearth and home goddess. The mistress and servants of each family take a sheaf of oats and dress it up in women's apparel, put it in a large basket, and lay a wooden club by it, and this they call Briid's-bed, and then they cry thrice, " Briid is come, Briid is welcome." Next morning they look in the ashes to see the impression of Briid's club there, and if they do they reckon it a true presage of a good crop and prosperous year, and the contrary they regard an ill omen. Shrove Tuesday was a great day in the Highlands for cock-fighting; then each scholar brought cocks to fight and decide who should be king and queen of the school for the ensuing year. It was also a noted day for ball-playing. Its popularity for nut-burning and marriage-divination by putting symbolic articles into brose or cakes is yet great.

CELTIC BURIAL RITES.

The customs at burial and the disposal of the dead among the early Celts can only be discovered in a general way. The earlier Aryan races evidently burned the bodies of the dead, preserved the bones in urns, and raised over them a circular mound. The poems of Homer present us with what may be regarded as typical examples of early Greek and Celtic burials. A pyre of wood was constructed and on the top of it the body was laid. Sheep and oxen were slain, their fat was placed about and upon the body, and their carcases were heaped around it. Jars of honey and oil were placed on the pile. Horses, favourite dogs, and captives were slain and cast on the pyre, and the whole set on fire. A wail was raised and the dead addressed by name. When the fire burned low, it was finally extinguished with wine, the bones were collected—" the whitened bones," as the poet says—and placed in an urn of gold. Then they dug a grave, and raised over it a mound. In historic times, in Greece and Republican Rome, the burning of the dead was the exception not the rule ; but in Imperial Rome the custom revived, and became the rule, while inhumation, at least of the better classes, was the exception, Christianity, however, finally stopped the burning of the dead. The old mounds had also developed into the elegance of built tombs, vaults, and monuments with inscriptions and other accessories of civilisation. Among the Celts of Gaul in Cæsar's time, evidently the Homeric age of burial was still prevalent; all the classical writers of that and the succeeding century testify to the burning of the bodies among the Gauls, but they are silent as to the character of the tombs. " Their funerals," Cæsar says, "are magnificent and costly, considering their civilisation ; and all that they think was dear to them when alive they put in the fire, even animals ; and shortly before this generation the slaves and dependents that they were considered to have loved, were burned along with them in the regular performance of funeral rites." Mela confirms this fully : " They burn and bury along with the dead whatever is of use to them when alive, and there were sone who, of their own free will, cast themselves on the funeral piles

of their relatives, expecting to live along with them."
Thus, we have not merely the burning of the bodies,
but also the burning of things useful in this life,
and more especially of slaves and relatives ; the
latter practice having become, previous to historic
times, obsolete. No trace of the remembrance of
a time when the dead were burnt can be found
in the earliest histories and myths of Ireland or
Britain, although abundance of instances occur
where personal and other property has been *buried*
along with the dead ; and even the immolation of
captives is not unknown, as when the Munster
hostages were buried alive around the grave of
Fiachra, about the end of the fourth century of our
era. Sacrifice of animals is referred to in the story
of Etain, the fairy queen of Eochaid Aiream, who
was left to " dig the *Fert* (grave), to raise the wail,
and slay the quadrupeds," for Ailill the king's
brother. Burial of arms is mentioned more than
once ; an old " Druidic " poem celebrates the fall
of Mog-Neid, King of Munster in the second century
of our era ; it says—

> " The grave of Mog-Neid is on Magh Tualaing,
> With his lance at his shoulder,
> With his club, so rapid in action,
> With his helmet, with his sword."

The Scottish Gaelic " Lay of Dargo " presents us
with a much more touching and important instance
of devotion than any of these. Dargo's wife expressed her love for her husband when the concocted

story of his death was brought to her, the effects
of which killed her, in these words—

> " Chi mi 'n seobhag, chi mi 'n cù
> Leis an d'rinn mo rùn an t-sealg,
> 'S o na b'ionmhuinn leis an triùir,
> Càirear sinn 'san ùir le Dearg."

> I see the hawk, I see the hound,
> With which my love performed the chase,
> And as the three to him were bound,
> Let us in earth with Dearg have place.

What kind of tomb was erected over them ?   In
answer to this question, we are at once referred to
the numerous barrows and tumuli scattered over the
country, and more especially in Ireland, where the
remarkable mounds on the Boyne could not fail to
attract the attention of all ages. " The traditions
and history of the mound-raising period have in
other countries passed away," says Standish O'Grady
very truly ; " but in Ireland they have been all
preserved in their original fulness and vigour, hardly
a hue has faded, hardly a minute circumstance has
been suffered to decay." A proud claim is this,
and one which for the very uniqueness among the
nations that it postulates for Ireland, invites criticism
and suspicion. The Euhemerist historians and
scribes of Ireland have woven an intimate chain of
connection between every event of their modest (!)
four thousand years' chronology and the topography
of their country ; be it the fortunes of Cesair before
the Flood, or of Partolan immediately after, or of

Brian Boromh a generation or two before the writer's time, yet every event is chronicled with a minuteness of genealogy, detail, and localisation that is quite oblivious of the perspective of time, the long roll of ages with their change of customs, and the uncertainty as to the far distant past. We saw that the Irish gods were changed to kings ; nay, more, their tombs can still be seen on the banks of the Boyne ! There are the barrows of the Dagda and his heroes, and there, too, Cuchulain rests beneath his mound. But just about his time Eochaid Aiream had introduced the practice of simple burial beneath the earth, and had abolished the old custom of burying the dead " by raising great heaps of stones over their bodies." These barrows are, mythologically considered, pre-Celtic ; they are beyond the ken of Irish history and myth, just as much as the Cromlechs are, which popular archæology accounts for as the " Beds of Diarmat and Grainne " or " Granua's Beds "—the beds occupied by this pair in their flight before Finn. Considered, again archæologically, they belong also to the races that preceded the Celts, as the character of the interments and of the accompanying articles proves. We have, however, continued reference in the myths and tales to the burial of early Christian times—the grave, the stone over it, and the inscription. How little the Irish writers understood the change of customs wrought by time is seen in the description by an Irish writer of the 12th century of the burial of Patroclus at Troy ; Achilles " built

his tomb, and he set up his stone and wrote his name."
Homer's account has already been given.   The Irishman described the custom of his own time as existing
in the time of the Trojan War.

THE "DRUID" CIRCLES.

First published, in book form, by Eneas Mackay, 1917.

First published in the Transactions of the Gaelic Society of Inverness, Volume XI., 1885

DRUID TEMPLE FROM THE NORTH.

THE "DRUID" CIRCLES.*

THE circles of rude, undressed stones found in various parts of the British Isles have been for the last two centuries alike the puzzle and the contention ground of archæologists. At the present time, the theories as to their origin and use are at least as numerous as the individuals who treat of them ; and, in such a chaos of opinions, a rational conclusion is difficult of attainment. Much, however, has been done during the last quarter of a century in clearing up the beliefs and customs of primitive man, and more accurate knowledge has been obtained about modern savages : in fact, a new science has been added to the many other " ologies," this one being called Anthropology—the science of man and civilisation. Much has also been done in settling the leading points of European ethnology ; for the science of language has been accepted as the basis and main source of study in tracing the affinity of the nations of Europe, and the result is that the leading facts of the ethnology of Europe are known and " fixed." In regard to the British Isles, quite a small revolution has occurred since the publication of Mr. Elton's

* The drawings of Druid Temple, Clava Cairns—north and south, and the northern cairn of Clava are from original etchings by Mr. Smart, who gave valuable assistance and suggestions throughout.

work on the " Origins of English History," where the
ethnology of Britain is dealt with in the light of all
the modern researches on ancient institutions,
history, language, and antiquities—whether human
crania or human works of art and use. From all
these scientific sources we are enabled to cast a
reflective light upon the darkness that shrouds
the so-called Druid circles and their builders. The
cause of failure in the usual theories is a common
one ; *a priori* conceptions are formed as to the
builders and the purpose of the circles, and the facts
are made unmercifully to square with such ideas.
And, further, archæologists are unfortunately too
apt in their eager pursuit of relics and remains, to
forget the living savage examples, and to ignore
the labours of students of savage and barbaric
beliefs and customs.   They in fact ignore the anthropologist ; and, what is more, they show too often
a very irritating ignorance and unappreciation of
the facts established by the science of language,
which has so revolutionised our conceptions upon
European ethnology.

I intend dealing with the question of the Druid
circles from an anthropologist point of view, and my
argument will run in two main lines, positive and
negative.   The positive argument will, after a general
description of the characteristics and geographical
distribution of stone circles, consider the history
and tradition in regard to them, and then inquire
if any such or similar structures are set up or used

now-a-days anywhere, and, if so, what their purpose
is. The negative side of my argument is the most
important ; here I will endeavour to prove who did
not build them, and what they were *not* built for,
an argument on the lines of elimination, for which I
will lay under contribution what modern research—
so far as is known to me—has done in unravelling
the early history of Europe and of the races that
successively were prominent there.

The stone circles consist of undressed stones, more
or less pillar-shaped, set on end in the circumference
of a circle. That is the only general statement that
can be made about them, for they continually differ
as to the size, interval, and number of stones in the
circle ; as to the size or number of circles, concentric or adjacent ; and as to the existence of other
structural accompaniments, such as outside trenches,
cairns or mounds inside, dolmens or menhirs at or near
the centre, or avenues of stones leading to them. The
size of the stones may vary from two dozen to only
one or two feet high ; the stones may be closely
set together or wide apart—thirty feet apart, as
some Inverness-shire circles have them. The diameter may vary from the twelve hundred feet of
the great Avebury circle to a few feet, and there may
be groups of circles together, or, as in the Inverness-
shire circles, the typical examples may consist of
three concentric circles, and so on. The structural
accompaniments — the dolmens, mounds, and
avenues—may appear each alone with them, or

together with one or more of the others. And in regard to their geographical distribution, they exist on the continent of Europe, more especially in Scandinavia ; they are numerous in Asia—in India, in Tartary, and especially in Arabia ; they appear also in North Africa, where fine specimens are found in Algeria and Tripoli ; but their most characteristic development is in Britain and Ireland, and in Britain, Scotland possesses the best examples, and again, of the Scotch circles, the Inverness and Inverness-shire ones are undoubtedly the best. The valley of the Nairn is the richest spot in Scotland for such remains.

Let us pass from these general statements to particular facts. The stone circle may exist alone : there are many examples of single stone circles unaccompanied by any other structure or super-structure. Such exist in Africa, India, Arabia, and frequently in the British Isles. These were alone and single from the first ; they did not get so through the denudations caused by time. But the general rule is to find with these circles other structural forms. Mr. Fergusson, who has written a most able, though prejudiced, work on " Rude Stone Monuments," considers the mound as architecturally the first step in the development of these monuments, and, for the mere explanation of terms, we may accept his order of exposition. The mound would require a row of stones round its base to keep it together ; hence arose the circle of close-fitting

CLAVA CAIRNS

GROUNDPLAN
SCALE $\frac{1}{100}$ inch to foot.

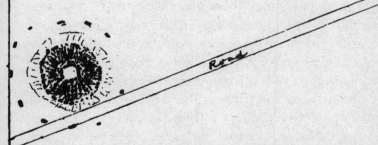

Road

Scale $\frac{1}{50}$ inch to foot.

SECTION THROUGH NORTHERN CAIRN TRANSVERSE TO PASSAGE

SECTION THROUGH MIDDLE CAIRN FROM W.S.W.

stones, which so often accompanies mounds and
cairns, and which sometimes also appears alone,
though not so often.   These mounds may be of
earth or stone, and their purpose is, as a rule, for
burial, though cairns might have also been raised
for the sake of " remembrance," " witness," and
boundary marks.   The burial mound or barrow may
have a cist in it—that is, four slabs of stone set in
box form, and with another slab super-imposed.
These cists were intended to receive the bodies or
the urns.   The cists when exposed, that is when
the earth of the mound is all cleared away, appear
as a box of large slabs, with a slab covering it ;
and this description, with the addition that the stones
are large, or megalithic, is true of a perfect " dolmen "
or " cromlech."   The dolmen consists of at least
two supporting stones and one covering stone, but
it usually has side stones as well as end stones.   The
true dolmens are found unattended by any trace of
tumulus, which shows that they were erected independent of any mound or cairn.   Nevertheless,
the best antiquarians are of opinion that they were
intended for burial purposes, and not for altars of
worship, as the " Druid " theorists have held.
Whether they were a development from the stone
cists is, perhaps, an open question.   Another feature
of certain barrows is the internal chamber.   This
chamber is generally circular, and built by over-
lapping the stones at a certain height, and thus
gradually narrowing the circle until at last the apex

of the chamber can be closed with one slab. The chambered cairns at Clava will illustrate the principle of this construction. Here there is a foundation laid of very large stones—some three feet high, and on this a course or two of stones is laid, not perpendicularly as is more usual, but with a backward inclination. At from four to five feet high, the stones begin to overlap all round until, at last, at a height probably of eleven or twelve feet, the circle could be closed by a single stone, thus forming a domed chamber, of a dozen feet in diameter and height. Leading to this chamber there may be a passage made of two walls of stone, with slabs across. The foundation-stones of the passage are usually large—megalithic, in fact. Now, two points are to be noticed here, according to the theory of the architectural development of these structures maintained by Mr. Fergusson : If the cairn or mound is removed, leaving only its megalithic foundations, there remain an interior circle of closely-placed stones, with an "avenue" leading into it. Hence the avenue or alignment of stones may be regarded as a development of the passage into the chamber of the mound, at least from an architectural point of view. These avenues of stone are common in France, but we have a good specimen of them in Lews, where at Callernish, we find an avenue of megalithic pillars—stones six or seven feet high on the average, leading to an interior circle of 42 feet diameter. The peculiarity at Callernish is that there branch

off from the circle three lines of stones, making, with
the avenue, a kind of cruciform groundplan.   The
great chambered mound at New Grange, in Ireland,
is entered by a long passage three feet wide and some
six feet high, the sides of which are composed of
megalithic pillars covered over with slabs.   The
chamber has branches running off right and left,
and a third in continuation of the passage.   The
general resemblance of this groundplan to that of
Callernish caused Dr. Stuart, in his "Sculptured
Stones of Scotland," to say : " If the cairns at New
Grange were removed, the pillars would form another
Callernish."   But Callernish was never covered
with a mound ; it was, indeed, threatened to be
covered with peat, accreted through countless centuries.   The avenue is too broad—eight feet broad—
and the stones too pointed to be covered with cross
slabs, while they stand apart from one another at a
distance of some six feet, and not close together,
as such a theory would require.   Besides, where
would the mound material be taken to in such a
place ?   Callernish, from these and other considera-
tions, was never even intended to be covered with
a mound or cairn.   These avenues attain their
highest development when unattended with any
other structures or superstructures in the way of
circles or of mounds, as at Carnac, in France.   Another accompaniment of the stone circle may be a
single standing stone or " menhir," placed either
interior or exterior to it.   And, lastly, we may men-

tion the existence of a ditch or trench exterior to a circle or to a mound. Such ditches have passages leading across them—a fact which throws some light on the passages of the Clava middle cairn. Specimens of these are to be seen in Derby and Cumberland. To sum up, we find circles connected with mounds, either inside the mound, round its base, or at a distance outside ; we find circles connected with or surrounding dolmens, whether mound-covered or not—some dolmens, as in India, being, indeed, on the top of the mound ; we find circles with avenues leading into them, and we find them with menhirs and with trenches. And there may be a combination of two or more of these along with circles. Further, it is amply clear that circles, avenues, dolmens, and menhirs were set up independent of any earth mounds or cairns.

A more particular description of the Invernessshire stone circles will tend greatly to elucidate the subject, more especially as the circles are so numerous, so well preserved on the whole, and so definite in their character and development. The Inverness and Strathnairn circles have been exhaustively mapped and described by Mr. Fraser, C.E., of Inverness, in a paper to the local Field Club, and to him I am in the main indebted for measurements and details. There are altogether twentyfive circles, more or less preserved, within the watershed of the Nairn, and some twelve or fourteen between that and the River Ness, and extending

as far as Loch Ness. The principal stone circles
and remains are at Tordarroch, Gask, Clava, Newton
of Petty, Druid Temple, and Dores. The general
characteristics of these circles are these :—(1) They
consist of three concentric rings of undressed boulder
or flag stones, fixed on end ; (2) The outer ring varies
in diameter from 60 to 126 feet—averaging 96 feet,
and consists of long stones, from nine to twelve in
number, set at nearly regular intervals, the tallest
being at the south side, and the size gradually
diminishing towards the north side of the circle ;
(3) The middle ring varies from 22 to 88 feet—
average being 53 feet—in diameter, and consists of
smaller boulders—few flags being used—set on end
close together, with a slight slope towards the centre
of the circle, and their best and flattest face outward.
The largest stones are here again on the south side,
and the smallest on the north ; (4) A third and central ring, concentric with the other two, from 12 to
32 feet in diameter—averaging 19 feet—consists of
stones or flags set on end close together. Of course
the accuracy of the concentricity of the circles cannot
be depended on ; they are often slightly eccentric.
They are built on low-lying or flat ground as a rule,
and where stones are abundant. An entrance
or " avenue " to the inmost ring can be distinguished
in four or five cases only, and its direction varies
from s. 5° E. to s. 41° w., the average direction being
that of the sun at one o'clock. It is only at Clava,
and only in two cases there, that chambers are found

constructed on the innermost ring, and bounded by the middle ring. But three others present traces of a cairn of stones having existed between the middle and innermost rings, which we may call ring cairns, but no sign of an entrance passage ; while two which have an avenue or passage (Croftroy and Druid Temple) do not present any clear traces of ever having had a cairn — certainly not the Druid Temple circles. As to the process of building them, it would seem as if the outer ring was set up first, and the other two rings thereafter, while any chambered or ring cairn would be built on these as a foundation.

Another interesting series of stone circles exists in Badenoch and Upper Strathspey. The principal circles are at Delfoor, Ballinluig, Aviemore, and Tullochgorm—half-a-dozen altogether. They all partake more or less of the ring cairn type ; there is an outer circle from 70 to 101 feet in diameter ; a middle one from 40 to 62 ; and an inner with a diameter varying from about 12 to 25 feet—average, 20 feet. The outer ring is in every case unfortunately incomplete, but it appears to average ten or eleven stones, the largest of which, some nine feet high, are to the south, and the lowest on the north side. The circle at Grainish, two miles north of Aviemore Station, is typical of the rest, and, indeed, typical of all these ring cairns. This circle has been known for a century or more. " Ossian " Macpherson, and his other namesake, Rev. John Macpherson, speak of it as " Druidic," and in this the historian

of Moray, Lachlan Shaw, agrees with them. Dr.
Arthur Mitchell describes it in the tenth volume
of the Society of Antiquaries' Transactions, but
gives an inaccurate idea of it in his drawing. The
outer ring, 101 feet in average diameter, is represented by two fallen stones—9 and 7 feet long respectively, while five others can be detected by their
fragments and the holes in the ground where they
stood. The stones themselves, being granite, were,
of course, appropriated for building purposes at no
very remote date. The second circle is, with the
exception of a gap or two, complete. The heaviest
stones are to the south, and it is the same with the
inmost circle. The middle circle has diameters
of 62 and 59 feet, while the inner has a uniform diameter of 25 feet. The cairn has fallen to some extent
into the internal open space. The depth of the
cairn is about four feet, and that also is the height
of the highest stones of the second ring. There is
no trace of any passage entering to the interior open
space through the ring cairn, any more than there is
trace of such in the Inverness circles, of the same ring
cairn kind at Clava, Culdoich, and Gask. It is, moreover, abundantly clear that this cairn was never
much other than it is now ; there never was a chamber erected on the innermost circle, for, were this so,
the stones would undoubtedly have still remained,
as the place is a long way from cultivated land, and
from any habitations. Within thirty yards of it,
to the south, there is a low barrow, enclosed by a

circle of small stones ; it is quite round, and 18 feet in diameter. There are several such around here, not far from the circles, all partaking of the same type. Most of them have been disturbed. The Strathspey Gaelic name for these stone circles and cairns is " Na carrachan," which implies a nominative singular " car," evidently from the same root as *cairn*.

The examination and study of these Inverness-shire circles and rude stone monuments raise the most important questions as to the intention and the plan of construction of stone circles. The three concentric circles seem developed, architecturally speaking, from the chambered cairn, encircled at its base, and with another circle at a distance. The next step would seem to have been the ring cairn. Possibly the reason for the ring cairn may consist in the fact that the builders could not, on their bee-hive system, and with the stones they used, as seen in the chambered cairns at Clava, construct chambers on so large a diameter as all the undoubted ring cairns have in their innermost circle, such as those of Clava, Gask, Grainish, and Delfoor, all of which are over 20 feet in diameter. The third step might have been to drop the building of the ring cairn, which would thus leave the three concentric circles, so peculiar in their character, in that they have a middle circle evidently designed for forming an outer ring intended to bound a cairn so as to keep it together. Druid Temple at Leys, Inverness,

CLAVA CAIRNS—NORTH AND SOUTH

presents a good example of stone circles evidently not completed by cairn of any kind, and yet having traces of avenue, which so few of them have. It also shows the state of preservation in which the ravages of time and the last century or two of stone-building have left these monuments of a remote antiquity.

In regard to the purpose of building these structures, the answer which the interrogation of them gives to the inquirer depends mainly on his individual theories. The construction of the central and middle circle, I believe, is developed from the chambered cairn, but it is in regard to the outer circle that the real difficulty exists. What is the purpose of it ? The chambered cairns are, by most antiquarians, connected with burial, though other theories, as we shall see, are held. In any case, burial deposits and urns were found in the Clava chambered cairns, a fact which connects them somehow with burial. It does not appear that the other circles have been yet scientifically explored ; at any rate burial deposits have not been found, except in the doubtful instances of Druid Temple and Gask. An urn was found in a gravel cutting near the former, and bits of bone have been found in the debris which lies in the interior of the latter.

In Ireland, besides the famous mound of New Grange, with its surrounding circle of monoliths, and the several other mounds on the Boyne, where, according to old Irish history, repose the fairy heroes of Ireland's golden age—the Dagda and his compeers, in whom modern research recognizes the old deities of the Gael—besides these there are the " battle-fields " of the two Moyturas, the " tower fields " as the name means, which are literally strewn with circles, mounds, and stones. The stone circles here are often alone, and often in connection with the mounds, cairns, and dolmens. It was on these Moytura plains that the fairy heroes overcame their foes of ocean and of land—the Fomorians and the Fir-bolgs ; so Irish history says, and the dates of these events are only some nineteen centuries before our era !   In England, several good specimens of stone circles still remain in the remote districts, such as Cornwall and Cumberland ; they are often single circles unattended by any other structure ; but there is a tendency towards their existing in groups, some circles intersecting one another even— such groups as at Botallick in Cornwall, Stanton Drew in Somersetshire, and others. The most famous stone monuments in England, or in these Isles, are those of Stonehenge and Avebury. The remains at Avebury, from the immense size of the outer circle (1200 feet) and its external rampart, its remains of two sets of contiguous circles, each set being formed of two concentric rings of stones, and its two remarkable avenues of stone, each of more than a mile in length, the one winding to the south-east, the other to the south-west—these remains have brought Avebury into rivalry with Stonehenge, with which it contests the honour of having been,

as some think, vaguely heard of by the Greeks before
the Christian era. Stonehenge, however, though
much less in extent—its outer circle is only 100 feet
in diameter, which is just about the average of the
outer circles of Inverness-shire—is much better
preserved and much better known. It differs in
various ways from the usual type of circles and their
accompaniments, though preserving the general
features. In the first place the stones are " dressed "
so far as to render them more suitable for contact
with, or superimposition of, other stones. Stonehenge
is, therefore, not quite a " rude stone monument."
This dressing of the stones was connected with
another, though less unique, feature of these circles.
This is what is known as the trilithons. These
are composed of two upright pillar stones set
somewhat apart, with another stone passing on the
top from the one to the other. The trilithon is
common in Asiatic monuments, but not in European,
and Mr. Fergusson is of opinion that, architecturally,
it is only an improved dolmen, standing on two legs
instead of four. An earthen vallum surrounded
the outer circle at a distance from it of 100 feet
The outer circle itself was 100 feet in diameter, and
consisted originally of thirty square piers, spaced
tolerably equally ; but only twenty-six of these can
now be identified, in whole or part. They were,
evidently, all connected by a continuous stone
impost or architrave, of which only six are now in
position. Passing over the smaller and more

doubtful second circle, we come to the five great trilithons, the plan and position of which are now quite settled. Their height is from 16 to 21 feet. high. They form a horse-shoe plan, two pairs on each side, and one pair at the middle of the bend. Inside this inner circle or horse-shoe are ten or eleven stones, more or less *in situ ;* they are of igneous rock, such as is not to be found nearer than Cornwall or even Ireland. The highest is over 7 feet, but the others are generally smaller. They seem to go in pairs about 3 feet apart, and may have formed the supports of trilithons. Between the outer circle and the great trilithons there are the remains of another circle of stone, some 5 feet high, and if it was complete—which is doubtful, it would consist of over forty stones, of which only some sixteen remain. Within the inner horse-shoe there is a stone in a recumbent position, called the " Altar " stone, but whether its proper place was here or elsewhere we cannot now say. Excavations inside the Stonehenge circles have led to no satisfactory conclusion, because they were instituted too long ago, first in 1620 ; and, though bones and armour are mentioned, we cannot say whether the bones were human or the armour of iron. Fragments of Roman and British pottery have been found in it ; but the best antiquaries are of opinion that the circles belong to the Bronze Age, and to a late period even in it. Bronze Age barrows surround it, belonging, as is shown by the chippings of the igneous stone of the inmost circle, to the same age as the megalithic monument itself. But there are also barrows of older tribes around and near it. " There are indications," says Mr. Elton, " that the people of the Bronze Age were the actual constructors of the temple on a site which had previously been selected as a burial-ground for the chieftains of the Neolithic tribes."

The only other stone circles I shall allude to, are those of Palestine and Arabia, and of these I shall speak only of those of the desert of Sinai and of the land of Moab. The explorations of the Ordnance Survey in 1869 have made the antiquities of the Sinai region perfectly known to us. Besides the ordinary bee-hive house of the Scotch type, there are also circles " nearly identical in character with those which in England and Scotland are commonly called Druidical Circles." They consist, as a rule, of a single outer ring of large standing stones, from 3 to 4½ feet high, and placed in contact with one another ; in some cases there is an inner concentric ring. The outer ring varies in size from 10 to 50 feet in diameter. In the centre of each circle a cist about 4 feet long by 2½ feet wide and deep is found, with its sides composed of four large stones, and the top covered over with a heavy slab, which is generally level with the surface. The corpse was placed in this cist on its left side with the knees bent up to the chin. Over the cist is placed a small cairn, enclosed by a ring of standing stones of smaller size than those

in the outer circles. " None of the cists," says
Major Palmer, " opened by the Sinai expedition
contained anything in addition to the skeleton,
except in one instance, when some marine shells
and worked flints were found," though other ex-
plorers found a lance and arrow-heads of flint in
another. In only one case were these circles found
associated with the bee-hive houses, and opinions
differ as to whether the same race built them both,
though they are all agreed that these remains are
pre-historic—built by a people antecedent to the
Jews, and the rest of the Semites, and long anterior
to the Exodus. In regard to the Land of Moab,
Canon Tristram says : " In Moab are three classes
of primæval monuments : stone-circles, dolmens,
and cairns, each in great abundance in three different
parts of the country, but never side by side. The
cairns exclusively range in the east, on the spurs of
the Arabian desert ; the stone circles, south of
Callirrhoe ; and the dolmens, north of that valley.
The fact would seem to indicate three neighbouring
tribes, co-existent in the pre-historic period, each
with distinct funeral or religious customs. Of
course, the modern Arab attributes all these dolmens
to the Jinns."

What, then, is the origin and history of these stone
circles ? We may apply to history, to etymology,
and to tradition in vain. The historians of the
ancient world took practically no notice of them.
Cæsar may have stood among the pillared stones of

Carnac, watching the fight between his fleet and that of the Veneti, but, as these monuments did not interfere with his martial or political designs, he, as is his wont, makes no reference to them. Diodorus Siculus, quoting from older sources, makes a wild reference to " an island over against Celtica (Gaul), not less in size than Sicily, lying under the Polar Bear, and inhabited by the Hpyerboreans, so-called because they lie beyond the blasts of the north wind . . . . . Wherefore the worship of Apollo takes precedence of all others, and from the daily and continuous singing of his praises, the people are, as it were, his priests. There exists in the island a magnificent grove (temenos) of Apollo, and a remarkable temple of round (dome) shape, adorned with many votive offerings." This very unsatisfactory passage was greedily seized upon by those that favoured the " Druidic " origin of the stone circles, but it may be doubted if the island referred to was Britain at all—for Diodorus knew Britain perfectly well, and would have likely told us so, if this Hyperborean island was the same as Britain. And again, no people is more mythical than these Hyperboreans or dwellers beyond the North wind· The temple, too, was not merely round ; it was also dome-shaped, like the Gaulish and British houses. How far does this agree with Stonehenge ? It is useless to build or prop any theory on such a passage as this. In the 5th century, and on to the 11th century, we meet with constant edicts of church

councils against worship and sacrifice upon stones—
even the stones themselves were objects of worship.
In 452, the Council of Arles decreed that " if, in any
diocese, any infidel lighted torches or worshipped
trees, fountains, or stones, he should be guilty of
sacrilege." Stones, trees, and fountains form the
continual burden of these edicts. This worship
of stones and sacrifices upon them we need not
connect with stone circles, for there is no detail given
as to the character of the worship or the monuments
worshipped, or at which worship took place. It is
very probable, however, that the stones referred to
were those on the graves and around the mounds
of the dead. Ancestor worship was strong among
Celt and Teuton, and we know from old Norse
literature that the family tumulus or hòwe was not
merely a place of worship, but also a place of council.
In the Land-nama-bok, we read that at one place
" there was a harrow (' high place ') made there,
and sacrifices began to be performed there, for they
believed that they died into these hills." The use
of these howes, as places of meeting, and in villages
as places of festive resort, whereon the May-pole
tree might flourish, will also explain why the stone
circles were used, at least on two historic occasions,
in Scotland as places of solemn meeting. In 1349
the Earl of Ross and the Bishop of Aberdeen met
at the standing stones of Rayne, and in 1380, Alexander, " Wolf of Badenoch," summoned to meet him
at Rait, near Kingussie, the Bishop of Moray, who

CLAVA—NORTHERN CAIRN—INTERIOR OF CHAMBER.

protested against the proceedings, " standing outside
the circle." A remarkable reference to stone idols
occurs in a very old Irish manuscript as an incident
in the life of St. Patrick. When the Saint came to
Magh Slécht, the plain of adoration, there he found
Cenn or Crom Cruaich, the chief idol of Ireland,
covered with gold and silver, and twelve other idols
covered with brass. Patrick aimed at it with his
crozier, which caused it to " bow " to one side, and
the mark of the crozier was still to be seen on it when
the pious Middle Age scribe was writing, and the
earth also swallowed up the twelve idols as far as
their head, and there they were as a proof of the
miracle some six centuries later. This story may be
merely a mythical explanation of a circle of stones,
existent at Magh Slécht. The building of Stonehenge is doubtless referred to by Geoffrey of Monmouth, who says that Merlin transferred the stones
from Ireland and set up the circles in England as a
monument over " the consuls and princes whom the
wicked Hengist had treacherously slain," as Scotch
legend represents the Cummings to have slain the
Mackintoshes or Shaws at the feast. Stonehenge
attracted attention after the revival of learning
set in with the Reformation. King James I. interested himself in its origin and history, and got
plans made of it by his architect, Inigo Jones. Jones
ascribed it to the Romans, and immediately another
set it down as of Danish origin. Aubrey and
Stukeley afterwards started the theory that it was a

temple of Druidic worship. Toland clenched this
with all the scholarship he could command, and not
merely claimed Stonehenge and such like structures
as Druidic, but all pre-historic cairns, dolmens,
as well as circles and single stones were made places
of Druidic worship. And from that time till a
generation or two ago the Druidic theory held almost
unquestioned sway.

The foregoing account is all that history can say
of the rude stone monuments of Europe ; Roman
and Greek history know them not—we except the
Cyclopean tombs of Mycenæ and their mythic history ; and even the references in early Christian
times are too vague to be of any satisfactory use ;
and should we grant the stone monuments mentioned
to be the rude stone circles, we could not be sure that
the Celts and Teutons of the 5th to the 11th centuries were using them for their primitive purpose.
In Asiatic history, these monuments fare no better.
Old Jewish history refers several times to altars of
rude stones and to stone monuments set up for remembrance of events, and for witness of compact ;
but, when closely examined, these accounts refer to
little more than a second-hand use of the pre-Jewish
monuments, or give merely a popular explanation
of the cairns and monuments of some long antecedent race.

Popular tradition and the examination or
etymology of the names applied to these rude stone
monuments yield even worse results than historical

investigation. One thing is to be noted ; popular tradition knows nothing of the Druids in connection with these circles. The nearest approach to the Druidic theory is where in one case the popular myth regards the stones as men transformed by the magic of the Druids. In fact, there is no rational tradition in regard to them. *They belong to a period to which the oldest tradition or history of the present race cannot reach.* For the accounts given of them are mythical, and the names given to them are either of the same mythic type, or are mere general terms, signifying cairns, stone monuments, or stone heaps. For example, the famous circles of Stanton Drew are said to have been a bridal party turned into stone ; a circle in Cornwall, which is called Dance Maine, or the dance of stones, is said to represent a party of maidens transformed into stone for dancing on the Sabbath day. We may learn from Giraldus that Stonehenge, or the " hanging stones," was known once as the Giants' Dance. In Brittany the avenues of Carnac are regarded as petrified battalions, and detached menhirs are their commanders, who were so transformed for offering violence to St. Cornily. These French groups of stones are variously attributed to the " unknown " gods ; the fairies and the devil get the best share of them, though extinct popular deities, like Gargantua, Rabelais' hero, may be met with. We meet with " Grottoes of the Feys," " Stones of the Feys," " Devil's Chair," " Devil's Quoits," " Staff of Gar-

gantua," and " Gargantua's Quoit." The covered
alleys or continuous cromlechs of Drenthe, in Hol-
land, are known as " Giants' Beds "—Hunebeds.
In Ireland, the cromlechs or dolmens are known as
the " Beds of Diarmat and Granua," or simple
" Granua's Beds "—the beds which this pair of lovers
made use of in their flight over Ireland when pursued
by Fionn. And it is here interesting to note, as so
far confirmatory of this worthy myth, that the
Arab shepherds of the present day recline on these
pre-historic dolmens and watch their sheep on the
plains. The tumuli are, of course, fairy mounds ;
the Gaelic name is *sithean*, a word derived from *sith*,
" fairy," allied to the Norse word *seithr*, " magic
charm." Single stones are variously accounted for ;
sometimes we meet with names indicative of worship,
" Clach   aoraidh "—worship   stone,   and   " Clach
sleuchda "—genuflection stone. But, as often as not,
the names have merely a reference to stones or stone
monuments ; as, for instance, already mentioned in
the case of Strathspey. The term *clachan*, as applied
to church in Scotch Gaelic, has been adduced as
proving that the churches are the descendants
of the stone circles where Druid worship was held ;
but it has first to be proved that the stone circles
are themselves known as the " clachans." The word
in Irish signifies hamlet, causeway, or grave-yard,
but it is also applied in an archæological sense to the
stone-built cells ascribed to the old Christian anchor-
ites, and its Scotch Gaelic meaning of church is

perhaps thence derived. How little it helps the
" Druid " theory is easy to see.

If history and tradition avail us not, let us see
whether any such rude stone monuments are set up
or used nowadays. If they are built and used by
any savage or barbarous tribe now, then it is more
than likely that the pre-historic builders of our stone
circles used them for similar purposes. Now we
do find that stone circles, if not built now, are at
least used now, and that rude stone monuments are
still being erected in India. With its 250 millions
of inhabitants, India is an epitome of the world ;
it contains every state of man and every stage of
belief—the oldest and the newest, Aryan and non-
Aryan. It presents us with nearly every form of
religion ; ancestor-worship, demon-worship, polytheism, Buddhism, Mohammetanism, and Christianity. It is among the non-Aryan tribes of the highlands of India that we must look for the most ancient
forms of worship. In the Dekkan we find rude stone
circles set up and still in use. Their use is for purposes of worship ; sacrifices are offered at the stones, and
the inner faces of the stones are daubed with patches
of red paint to denote blood, whereby they are consecrated to the deities. The victims sacrificed are red
cocks, and sometimes goats ; the blood of the sacrifice is consecrated to the deity invoked, but the flesh
is used by the votary himself. It would appear
that the number of stones in the circle had some reference to the number of families or individuals wor-

shipping there, and each stone appears to be the image or " fetish " of the particular deity worshipped. These deities are, therefore, all local and special, and as the Brahmins are opposed to the cult they ban it by every means in their power. These Dekkan rude stone monuments are not necessarily circular ; the stones may be arranged in lines or even irregularly, so that we cannot deduce much argument from the mere circular form of some of these monuments. We only note their religious purpose. And, again, in the hills of Assam we find rude stone monuments still set up, and probably their use bears more on our present inquiry than the circles of Dekkan. Among the Khasias, a barbaric tribe there, the worship of deceased ancestors prevails. They burn their dead and raise to their honour menhirs of stone either singly or in groups, but they do not arrange them in circles. The number of stones must be odd— 3, 5, 7, but also 10, if made into two fives. The worship, too, is of a very practical kind. If a Khasian gets into trouble or sickness, he prays to some deceased ancestor or relative, promising to erect a stone in his honour if he helps him—a promise which he faithfully performs, if the departed appears to have helped him. In regard to these Indian rude stone monuments and their bearing on European pre-historic ones, Mr. Tylor says : " It appears that the Khasias of north-east India have gone on to modern times setting up such rude pillars as memorials of the dead, so that it may be reasonably guessed that those of Brittany, for instance, had the same purpose. Another kind of rude stone structures well-known in Europe are the *cromlechs* (?) or stone circles formed of upright stones in a ring, such as Stanton Drew, not far from Bristol. There is proof that the stone circles have often to do with burials, for they may surround a burial mound or have a dolmen in the middle. But considering how tombs are apt to be temples where the ghost of the buried chief or prophet is worshipped, it is likely that such stone circles should also serve as temples, as in the case of South India at the present time, where cocks are actually sacrificed to the village deity, who is represented by the large stone in the centre of a cromlech (stone circle)." Such is Mr. Tylor's theory in regard to these structures, and that is the view of them which I shall endeavour to maintain and prove in this paper, while at the same time I shall further endeavour to make clear what races probably did build them and what races certainly did not.

Having now considered the character of the stone circles, their geographical distribution, their history as it presents itself in ancient authors and documents, their popular names and their mythic history in modern times, and having, lastly, discovered that rude stone monuments, and even stone circles are set up, and still used in India, and that their use there is in connection with religious rites, while, in Khasia, they were connected further with burial to a certain extent, let us briefly review the theories of the learned in regard to their purpose and use.   And, first, there comes the Druidic theory, started in the 17th century and still held by antiquaries of repute— men like Colonel Forbes-Leslie, who have done really admirable work.   The Druids were the priests of the Celts in Gaul and Britain.   They formed, if Cæsar may be trusted, a very powerful caste, matched only by the nobility ;   they   monopolised the power of judges, soothsayers, medicine-men, priests, edu- cationists, and poets.   Besides the ordinary poly- theism which they shared with Greece and Rome, the Druids believed in the transmigration of souls and theorised on the universe—its size and laws, and on the power and majesty of the gods.   Their position in Cæsar's Gaul looks like an anticipation of the Middle Age ecclesiastics.   We just know enough of these Druids to wish that we knew much more, but not enough to build much of a superstructure of religion and philosophy upon. Nevertheless, the meagre details that are left us so fired the imagination of some modern writers that a system of " Druidism " was attributed to the Celts, which in religious experience and philosophic breadth could rival any in the modern world, and far surpass any religion of antiquity.   The Druids officiated not merely in temples but in groves : this we gather from the classical authors.   Groves are retired spots, wood-surrounded, where no stones were necessary at all ; but what of the temples ? Now the Greek and Roman writers do not describe

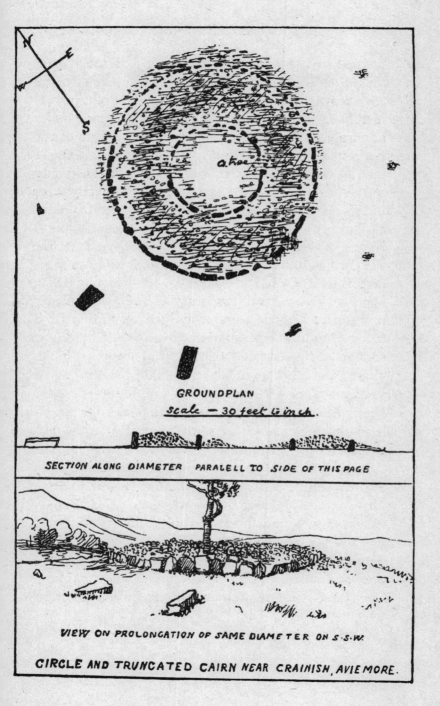

N
E
W
S

a tree

GROUNDPLAN
scale — 30 feet to inch.

SECTION ALONG DIAMETER PARALELL TO SIDE OF THIS PAGE

VIEW ON PROLONGATION OF SAME DIAMETER ON S.S.W.

CIRCLE AND TRUNCATED CAIRN NEAR CRAINISH, AVIEMORE.

any Celtic or Druidic temple, as far as I know ;
the inference from this might be that the Celtic
temples were like the Roman temples, or more
probably like the Celtic houses—" great houses,"
as Strabo says, " dome-shaped, constructed of
planks and wicker, with a heavy thatched roof."
The houses were wooden, except in the Gaulish
towns, and so would the temples be in rural districts
and in Britain, which was in a more primitive state
than Gaul in respect to towns. The Druidic argument may be put in this form—We are not told
what kind of temples the Celts and their Druids had ;
therefore, the Druids worshipped in the stone circles.
Or the matter may be put in this way—We know
but little of the Druids, and we know nothing of
the circles ; therefore, the Druids worshipped in the
stone circles. But why should they worship in
stone *circles ?* Well, the answer is this, as given
by the Druidic theorists : It is the solar circle—
these circles have a solar reference ; the sun was
worshipped in them. Others think these avenues
and circles are signs of a worship of snakes and
dragons, and the whole system of Baal-worship
and such like was transplanted from Phenicia and
Egypt into Gaul, and more especially into Britain.
Besides the fact that the Druidic argument proceeds
on vicious logical premises, I will later on prove that
Celtic priests could have nothing to do with the
building of rude stone circles. And if we look abroad
at the circles of India, Algeria, and Arabia, did the

the Druids also build them ? The Sinai circles, we saw, were extremely like the Scotch circles ; were there Celtic Druids in Sinai to erect them ? The theory that the circles were temples of Druidic worship fails therefore on two grounds : first, there is no evidence for it that can stand the test of scientific or logical investigation ; secondly, there is much positive evidence against it—the state of culture of the the Celts and the common connection of the circles with sepulture, for example.

The theory that finds most favour at the present day is that which connects the circles with the burial of the dead. The circles surrounded places of sepulture. We saw that the circles of Sinai were undoubtedly in connection with sepulture, and in regard to the circles in the British Islands, Mr. Fergusson says : " Out of 200 circles which are found in these islands, at least one-half, on being dug out, have yielded sepulchral deposits. One-half are still untouched by the excavator, and the remainder, which have not yielded their secret, are mostly the larger circles." He thinks it cannot be denied that circles up to 100 feet diameter are sepulchral, and if so, why should not the rest above that limit be so also ? Mr. Fergusson's estimate of the number of circles in the British Isles is far short of the truth ; there are over 200 circles in Scotland alone. This greatly weakens his argument on the proportion of sepulchral and non-sepulchral circles. Besides, it cannot be said that circles unaccompanied by any

mound, cairns, or dolmens have often yielded
sepulchral remains.   Yet with all these deductions,
there is a good deal of truth in the statement that
circles are connected with burial deposits, although
the proportion of actually found deposits is by no
means one-half nor anyways near it.   Now, supposing that we grant that these circles have always
or nearly always surrounded burial deposits, there
comes the question, still unanswered, what is the
object of a circle of stones *set at intervals* round a
burial.   Why should the *circular* form have been
adopted ?   And these questions the burial theory
cannot answer without further assumption, and it is
in regard to these assumptions that the best theorists
differ.

Mr. Fergusson's answer to these questions is, of
all the defenders of the " burial " theory, the most
satisfactory.   His opinion as to the architectural
development of the mound enclosing a body, into a
mound enclosing a cist, then into a mound enclosing
a chamber and having an outer circle of closely-set
stones to keep it together, has already been explained.
The bare foundations of such a chambered mound
would give two circles of stones, closely set together.
It is further probable that the megalithic foundation
was first laid down ; it appears, indeed, to have
been the custom in Homeric times first to mark out
the site of the tomb in somewhat of a circular or oval
form and then place stones round the outline ; and,
if that were so, may it not have dawned upon the

builders, so Mr. Fergusson suggests, what a pity it
was to hide away such handsome structures under a
mound of earth or cairn of stones ?   Added to this
may be taken the circumstance that some unfinished
mounds must have existed, which would still further
suggest the idea of leaving the mere foundation of
stones bare without any mound superimposed. Mr
Fergusson amply proves, in opposition to those
theorists who hold that all these structures, especially
dolmens, were once covered by mounds which the
progress of agriculture and building removed, that
such could not have been the case with most of
them.   An examination of our Inverness-shire
circles would show that many of them, such as
Druid Temple, were never anything but three
concentric circles, and never had a trace of mound
or cairn. Callernish is a standing disproof of this
theory, that circles and avenues are merely dismantled chambered cairns ; they may have been
uncompleted cairns, that is, cairns whose foundations
were laid, but they certainly were never covered
by stone or earth. Mr. Wakeman, the eminent
Irish archæologist, points out that not only were
dolmens and circles built bare—without super-
structure—but that, instead of the progress of time
and cultivation denuding them, they have actually
in many cases been covered with moss to a depth
which, from the well-known rate of growth of peat,
makes them at least some four thousand years old.
Mr. Wakeman also says : " From the stone cist

composed of four flag-stones set on edge and covered
by a fifth, to the spacious chambers found within
gigantic cairns like those of New Grange and Dowth,
through all peculiarities of size and structural com-
plication, we have for foundation simply the cromleac
(dolmen) idea." On Mr. Fergusson's development
theory we can account for two concentric circles
of closely set stones ; the megalithic foundation was
made to do duty for the mound ; we can also,
by this theory, account for their circular shape,
for a mound must be circular, and so must the bee-
hive chambers be also ; but, with all this granted,
how are we to account for the outer circle, which is
built round the tumulus or cairn, and at a distance
from it ? Clearly, the theory of architectural
development fails here, and Mr. Fergusson manfully
admits that it does. He suggests, with caution,
a possible resemblance in origin between them and
the rails of the Indian Buddhists—these rails being
composed of rows of tall stone pillars set at intervals
around the Buddhist dagoba. But as he says of
these Buddhist rails : " It is difficult to see what
these stone pillars or posts were originally intended
for," and suggests that it was for the hanging of
garlands, he does not help us much to an explanation
by this analogy. His other suggestion that these
stones, set at intervals, formed part of the outer
earthen rampart that surrounded the mounds at
first, and afterwards were retained on the disuse of
the vallum of earth, does not look so very happy

as the rest of his development theory, though it may fit in with the evolution of the inner circles from chambered mounds.

In refutation of any theory that would maintain that between these stones might have been built any earthen or wooden barrier, of which the stones would form the leading supports, we may adduce the fact that in the Inverness-shire circles the stones on the south are very tall, while those on the north side are very small, so small at times as to render such a use altogether impracticable.   On all theories in regard to the use of stone circles in connection with burials, Canon Greenwell, in his epoch-making book on " British Barrows," says : " It has been suggested by some that the enclosing circles were merely made to support the mound at its base. It is only necessary to remark, in refutation of this surmise, that the circle is often within the mound, is sometimes a trench, and is, as before mentioned, nearly always incomplete. Others have, and with more reason, supposed them to be marks of *taboo*, a fence to preserve the habitation of the dead from desecration, but the fact that so many are within, and must always have been concealed, by the barrow, appears to me to be inconsistent with this explanation.   I think it more probable, if the notion of a fence is to be entertained, that they were intended to prevent the exit of the spirit of those buried within, rather than to guard against disturbance from without.   A dread of injury by the spirits of the dead has been very commonly felt by many savage and semi-civilised peoples ; nor, indeed, is such fear unknown in our own times, and even amongst ourselves ; and it may well be that, by means of this symbolic figure, it was thought this danger might be averted, and the dead kept safe within the tomb." And we may add to the testimony of Canon Greenwell, that of Mr. Llewellyn Jewitt. In his work on " Grave-mounds," he distinguishes between the smaller circles which surround, or at one time surrounded grave-mounds, and the larger circles, which were probably, he thinks, for totally different purposes from the grave-mounds.

Another theory as to the purpose of these stone structures has attained some prominence lately. It is maintained that these circles are the foundations of the houses of the ancient inhabitants, and that the chambered cairns, like those of Clava, formed one class of dwelling-houses, while the outer circle may have been a wall of defence. But the houses built on these circles were, according to this theory, as a rule, brochs. Now, there are many remains of these brochs in Scotland, some of them fairly entire. Their construction is somewhat complex. The broch consists of a hollow circular tower, about 60 feet in diameter, and 50 feet high ; its wall may be about 15 feet thick ; and about 8 feet from the ground the wall is divided by a space of 2 to 3 feet into an outer and inner shell, and this space is divided vertically into a series of galleries by slabs run across all round the tower. Access is obtained by a single outside door into the interior, and thence by stairs up into the galleries. There may be a series of ground chambers in the wall at its base. Miss Maclagan, in her book on " Hill Forts," maintains that Stonehenge is practically the base of a broch ; the two outer circles form the foundation of the outer wall, while the two inner circles form the base of the inner wall—the great trilithons were merely doorposts and lintels. The theory is ingenious ; the brochs, if stripped to their megalithic foundations, would present an outer and inner ring, while the chambers at the base, if we assume these carried all round, would give two intermediate circles. But where is the stone material gone to in nearly every case ? It must be assumed here again, as in the " burial " theory, that the material has been all removed, or that only megalithic foundations were laid, and the work left incomplete. Then there are several practical objections ; these megalithic pillars are unsuited for foundation stones as they stand, and there is no trace of the outer circles having ever been anything else than they are now ; nor is it easy to see what practical use they could be put to in building or fencing. Burial deposits have been found in the chambered cairns, and within the circles, and this does not accord with their having been dwelling-houses. Miss Maclagan, however, has the usual argument in such cases—*argumentum ad ignorantiam.* The burials " belonged probably to

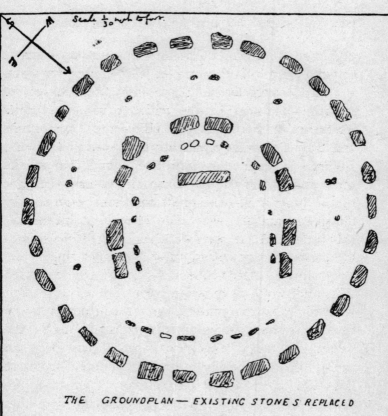

Scale ⅟₃₀ inch to foot.

THE GROUNDPLAN — EXISTING STONES REPLACED

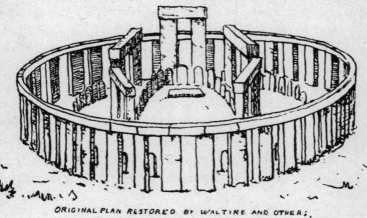

ORIGINAL PLAN RESTORED BY WALTIRE AND OTHERS.

STONEHENGE.

a comparatively recent date, and not to the original purpose of the structure." This has often undoubtedly happened, and we may quote one interesting case in the Sinai Desert—" In a great many cases," says Major Palmer, " the stone houses (of bee-hive form) have been converted into tombs by some later race, who, for this purpose, closed the doorways and removed the roof-stones, laying the corpses at full length on flat stones inside, heads to the west, and then covering them with earth and finally with stones, until the interior was filled up." And it may be further pointed out that probably the sepulchral chamber is but an imitation of the habitations of the living at the time. The chambered cairns at Clava may well have been copies of the dwellings of that day, but the badness of the masonry of the interior of the chamber forbids us thinking that they could have been used for the tear and wear of everyday life as dwelling-houses. " There certainly is a great resemblance," says Canon Greenwell, " between some of these receptacles for the dead, especially in Scandinavia, and the places of abode of the Eskimo and other Arctic residents."

Let us now consider a negative argument : What races in early Europe could not have been the builders ? Linguistic science has quite clarified our views as to the main features of European ethnology. We can prove from the languages of Europe the racial connection of the European nations as far as language is concerned, and that means a good deal more, for community of origin as regards language is followed by the same in regard to religion and institutions—political and social. A common language will not, of course, prove that nations are all descended from the same racial stock, for a superior race may impose upon a weaker or less civilised one its own language with consequent religion and customs. Language, therefore, is a test more of culture than of racial descent. Some four thousand years ago, more or less, a race now called the Aryan began in separate bands to impose upon the previous inhabitants its rule and its language, and the consequence has been that at the present time Europe is possessed by Aryan-speaking peoples, with the exception of unimportant remnants like the Basques and Finns, or late intruders like the Turks. The nations that existed before the Aryan supremacy were doubtless amalgamated, and their influence must be felt in national and tribal differences of physique, in the vocabulary and idiom of the present Aryan languages, and in the religious beliefs and the customs of the present races. May not also the monuments of their hands, built for their habitation, their religion, or their dead, still exist among us ? We shall see. The Aryan race had attained a certain high stage of culture. The state was founded on a patriarchal basis, and there were kings, and the family was the unit and starting point of the organisation ; monogamy was the rule ; agriculture was known ; they had towns and roads ;

metals were used, including the precious ones, and
the more useful, such as copper, tin, and bronze,
and, in over-running Europe, they had iron ; their
religion was polytheistic—the worship of the higher
objects of nature under anthropomorphic form,
with a strong admixture of ancestor-worship and
other lower forms. Of the Aryan races, the Celts
made their appearance in the West first, at the
dawn of history occupying Northern Italy, the
Upper Danube, Switzerland, France and the Low
Countries, most of Spain, and all Britain and Ireland.
The state of culture of the Celts we can discover
by their Aryan descent to a great extent, but as
they became modified through disseverance from the
rest, and through mingling with the pre-Celtic
peoples, we require to study every scrap of historical
reference we get, and also the inscriptions and other
monuments that remain to us of their ancient life ;
while we have also to study their language, their
customs, their oldest literary efforts, and their
mythic tales, legends, and histories. The study of
all these, steadied by a reference to the customs
and developments of races nearly akin, like those
of Rome and Greece, enables us to read the " weather-
worn " history of the Celts, and to know their state
of culture. Cæsar and the other classical writers
did not perceive their kinship with the Celts ; unless
when for political reasons the Senate might call
the Ædui " brothers and kinsmen," yet in their
descriptions they take some four-fifths of the facts

of their life, their habits, and their institutions, for granted as being much the same as existed in Italy and in Rome. Only the oddities, differences, and signs, of " barbarianism " were noted ; the points of coincidence were passed over as nothing to be wondered at, though these were generally the most wonderful facts of all. The Celtic race was in Cæsar's time in about as high a state of civilisation as the Romans were about the time of the Punic war a century and a half previous. They possessed a language of equal, perhaps superior, power to that of Rome ; they had political systems of the Grecian type before the supremacy of Athens ; and they must have had an enormous oral, and, possibly, written literature. In Gaul they built towns of the Roman type, with stone houses, temples, and such like ; but rural Gaul and Britain contented themselves with wooden houses and wooden fortifications—stockaded clearings or strong hill positions. They seem to have done little in stone buildings. They built temples ; but they *were* temples and not stone circles, which are not mentioned at all. Their temples could not have been much different in construction from those of the Greeks and Italians, otherwise mention would be made of the fact. The temples were of wood, like the houses, and, like the Northumbrian temple of Coifi, which was built like a house. The Greek writers use two words in their description of Celtic places of worship : these are *temple* and *grove* (temenos), or consecrated allotment.

The Celts buried their dead like the other Aryan nations ; they burnt the bodies, like the Greeks of Homeric times, and built the tumulus over the ashes, though it is just as likely that the common people buried by inhumation as in Greece and Rome. The tumuli, also, were erected only over chiefs and great men, as among the pre-historic and contemporary tribes. The Homeric burial existed, according to Roman and Greek writers, in Gaul. Homer represents Achilles as placing the fat of many sheep and oxen, whose carcases were heaped round the pyre, about the body of Patroclus, from head to foot. He set vessels with honey and oil slanting towards the bier, and then threw horses, pet dogs, and captive Trojans, after slaying them, on the pile, to be burnt along with the body of his friend. Celtic burial tumuli are not easy to identify. Burials of the pre-Roman and pre-Christian period of Celtic occupation are very few indeed, and in archæological works are continually confused as " Anglo-Saxon," being, indeed, of a similar type. Like their houses and temples, they were of no lasting character. One thing is clear : they had no rude stone circles around them.

The Celts made use of iron ever since they appear in history. It is not likely on *a priori* grounds that they would build *rude* stone circles for worship or even for burial, nor can it be understood from their religious beliefs what use they could make of *circles* of rude stone. The Druids again were

merely the Celtic priests—a priesthood of more than
ordinary influence and power, but their doctrines
contained little else than was believed in then by
other Aryan races in Europe or Asia. It is sheer
improbability that they could have worshipped
in stone circles.

If the Celts did not build these rude stone monuments, then some race previous to them, and in a
more barbaric state of culture, must have been the
builders. Various facts go to show that there existed
previous to the Celts another people or rather other
peoples. Professor Rhys has proved from the
evidence of language and mythology that there was
a previous race; while Mr. Elton, founding on a
study of customs and on the researches of archæologists, has still further proved the fact. Following
Canon Greenwell and Dr Thurnam, and extending
the significance of their conclusions, Mr. Elton
is able to prove that two races at least existed
previous to the Celtic race. There was, first, the
small, dark-skinned, long-headed race of the Neolithic
and later cave age, whom Mr. Elton calls Iberians,
whose descendants survived in Siluria of Wales,
in Ireland, and in Aquitania, and who spoke a language probably like the Basque. They were the
builders of the *oval* barrows. The second race was
tall, rough-featured, strong-limbed, round-headed,
and fair-haired, and Mr. Elton calls them Finnish
or Ugrian. They appear to have been in their
Bronze Age, whereas the Iberians were in their

Stone Age. The Finnish race may have had an alphabet, if we can attribute to them the numerous unreadable inscriptions--rock-carvings and sketchings of the Bronze Age—which appear in Ireland, Scotland, and Scandinavia. They appear to have subdued the previous race. They built the *round* barrows, and we have every reason to believe that they were also the builders of the rude stone *circles*, their crowning effort being the temple (?) of Stonehenge. We have besides their burial customs, glimpses possibly of their social condition. Cæsar and other writers continually and persistently refer to races in Britain who had community of wives, and there can be no question that there was some foundation for the rumour. Nor can we have much doubt that the nation referred to was this Finnish one, for it is quite certain that it was not a Celtic or Aryan nation, among whom monogamy was the strict rule. The Pictish custom of succession through the female also establishes among them low ideas of marriage, quite consonant with community of wives ; and from this we must conclude that the Picts were strongly intermixed with, if not altogether, a non-Aryan race. The nakedness and blue paint of historians is another feature which, as knowledge of the races of Britain advanced, the classical writers learned to locate among the inhabitants of Northern Scotland.

The long barrows were built by a race anterior to this Finnish race ; the Finnish race built the round

barrows, chambered cairns, and rude stone circles.
They were probably also the builders of the brochs.
The theory that brochs are of Norse origin arises
from ethnological confusion ; for the Norse were
Aryans possessing iron implements, and builders,
like the Germans and Celts, of wooden and not of
stone buildings. The Picts were Finnish. Mr.
Joseph Anderson says that stone circles attain their
principal' development in Pictland proper, and are
most abundant in the district between the Moray
Firth and the Firth of Tay.   " Those of the Scottish
circles that have been examined," he says, " have
yielded interments of the Bronze Age."   This better
development of the circles in Pictland goes to prove
that the circle builders lasted longer in Pictland
than anywhere else, and, in fact, that the builders
were the ancestors of the historic Picts, and possibly
the historic Picts themselves.   Mr. Fergusson, from
quite another standpoint, suggests that Clava is the
burial place of the royal family of Brude Mac
Maelchon, the king whom Columba visited on the
banks of the Ness. The suggestion is not at all
a bad one.

We shall now draw the threads of our argument
together. In our process of elimination we discovered that the Aryan races built no stone circles ;
the Celts, therefore, and their Druids, had nothing
to do with them ; they are pre-Celtic as well as pre-
historic ; the circles are so often connected with
burial that we may take it for granted that they all

VIEW IN KHASSIA HILLS

IN THE DEKKAN, NEAR ANDLEE

RUDE STONE MONUMENTS OF INDIA

originally had to do with burial ; but we found, also,
that in modern times, circles and stones were connected with worship, more especially the worship
of ancestors. Everything points to their having
been places of burial ; they surround dolmens and
barrows, or even when alone yield at times burial
deposits ; but their peculiar character, coupled with
the fact of modern and ancient worship of and at
stones, must make us pause ere we set burial down
as their sole purpose. Would savage or barbaric
man, out of mere reverence for the dead, raise such
monuments to their memory ? It remains to consider what kind of worship could be held at places
of sepulture, and why stone circles should be used.
In the matter of worship, the old theories as to the
sun and serpent worship may be dismissed as out of
place in connection with burial, for the worship of
the sun as the giver of light and heat has never
had connection with death ; Apollo must not be
contaminated with death. The evident reference
many of the circles have to the sun's course, as for
instance that in this district the heaviest stones
are to the south, or that the entrance may have a
southerly aspect, only proves that the light and heat
of the sun were regarded as necessary for the dead
as well. That the existence of solar worship would
add to and emphasise the " sunward " tendency—
the sun reference of the circles—is freely allowed,
but nothing more can be legitimately deduced from
such a fact. As for serpent worship, it is plain that

the advocates of that theory did not quite grasp the full significance of the serpent cultus and its connection with phallic worship. The only worship appropriate at the grave is that of deceased ancestors. A study of the beliefs and customs of savage and barbaric races makes it abundantly clear that this is about the earliest shape in which religion manifests itself. We must inquire what the anthropologist has to say in regard to people in this state of culture. Reverence for the dead and belief in the existence of the Deity are glibly asserted by theorists as existent among every race, but that is a delusion. Reverence and belief in the sense understood by a civilised and educated person there are none, for savage belief is eminently practical and unsentimental. To project the highest feelings and opinions of civilised man—and these local, too—into the early state of man, is to overlook the long perspective of time with its evolution of ever higher feelings and beliefs. The lowest phase of belief has been named by Mr. Tylor, " animism ; " it consists in believing that what is presented to us in our dreams and other hallucinations has a real objective existence. Savage man makes little or no difference between his dreaming and waking state. He sees the " shadows " of the dead in his sleep, and believes in their objective reality. But not merely the dead have shadows or spirits ; the living, too, have a spirit duplicate of self. The reflection in water proves this no less than the presentiment of the living man in dreams. Hence it is that the savage dislikes the photographer. Animals and material objects, of course, have souls, on the same grounds, for the dead hero appears in dreams with ghost of hatchet, sword, and spear. " The Zulu will say that at death a man's shadow departs and becomes an ancestral ghost, and the widow will relate how her husband has come to her in her sleep, and threatened to kill her for not taking care of his children ; or the son will describe how his father's ghost stood before him in a dream, and the souls of the two, the living and the dead, went off together to visit some far-off kraal of their people." The funeral sacrifices of historic nations, of early Greeks, Romans, and Celts, show how barbaric religion includes the souls of men, animals, and material objects ; for what was useful to the dead when alive was burnt or buried along with them—chariots, arms, horses, dogs, and even wives and slaves were sacrificed in one mighty holocaust. The religious creed in which " animism " embodies itself is, of course, the worship of the dead, especially the worship of ancestors. Worship and reverence, here, have a different sense from our ideas of them. The dead are worshipped for protection, and repaid with reverence, not merely in feeling, but also in practical gifts and sacrifices at their tombs. It may quite as often happen that their wrath is deprecated. From the mere family ancestor, the worship may rise to that of great chiefs and kings that are departed, and from that it

may rise to a conception of a supreme father—
" The old old one " of the Zulus, as they work
back from ancestor to ancestor, thus arriving at an
idea of a creator, akin to the conception of the
" Ancient of Days." One's own ancestor may be
good to one ; other people's ancestors may be the
reverse. Hence these last have to be propitiated ;
evil spirits are worshipped to avoid their wrath.
Thus the ghost of a British officer was not long ago
worshipped in India as a god, and on his altar his
demon-worshipping votaries placed what they
thought would please and appease him, for it had
pleased him in this life, namely, offerings of cheroots
and brandy ! In fact, all the ills that life is heir to
are among some races attributed to evil spirits,
while the good is the work of the beneficent spirits ;
and among such tribes it is through the medicine-
man, with his exorcisms, there is the only means of
escape. Let it be noted that ancestral ghosts may
not merely exist in proper human form, but they
often assume animal forms, and what is more, they
may even take up their abode in material objects—
trees, stones, or anything. Hence arises " fetish "
worship—the worship of " stocks and stones."
And it is also easy to see that we may, on the other
hand, rise from ancestor worship, through this
transmigration idea, to the height of polytheism,
with its gods of sun, moon, and sky.

This reverence of the savage for the dead is therefore connected with his regard for himself. His

religion, as usually happens in higher phases of culture, is selfish. The dead are therefore cared for and their abodes become places of worship. Various ways are adopted for disposal and worship of the dead. The hut they lived in may be left as a dwelling for them ; the body may be buried in a canoe or coffin ; a strong tomb may be built over it or its ashes, and this tomb may be a chamber with access to it to enable the votaries to bring offerings. Great labour was bestowed on these burial mounds of earth and stone. Nor have we yet ceased from this display, though we now have different methods and far different feelings in our burial rites. Yet there are survivals of ancient forms. " In the Highlands of Scotland," says Mr. Tylor, " the memory of the old custom [raising of mounds and cairns] is so strong that the mourners, as they may not build the cairn over the grave in the churchyard, will sometimes set up a little one where the funeral procession halts on the way." Our memorial stones over the graves are but the descendants of the old menhirs ; nor are dolmen forms absent in the stone box structures often placed over graves. In the Churchyard of Rothiemurchus, on the grave of Shaw Cor-fhiaclach, the hero of the North Inch at Perth, there used to be a row of small pillared stones set round all the sides of the tomb-stone. Circles of stone other than such far-off imitations as this we do not use now.

Burial and worship in early society go hand in

hand, and we, therefore, conclude that these stone circles were used for both burial and worship, but more especially for worship, since mere reverential memorials were, at that stage of culture, an impossibility. Nevertheless there yet remains one part of our inquiry to which an answer has not been given. Why should the stones be set up *at intervals*, and *in a circle ?* For all that our inquiry has proved is that the dead were worshipped at their *graves ;* it does not necessarily answer the more particular question of a peculiar form of grave or burial enclosure. The circular form and the pillared stones set at intervals remain, after every elimination, the only difficulty of the enquiry. Mr. Fergusson developed the idea of the circle from the circular mound, but he could not account for the stones being set at intervals, and not close together. Canon Greenwell suggested, as we saw, that their use was to " fence " in the ghost of the departed. It is a superstition in the Highlands yet that evil spirits can be kept off by drawing a circle round oneself. Another suggestion made is that the number of stones may have had something to do with the number of worshippers, as is said to be the case in the Dekkan. It was also the custom at the Hallowe'en fires for everyone to place a stone in a ring round the fire as they were leaving, and, if by next morning, anything happened to any of the stones, the person who placed it there was fated to meet death or ill during the year. The Arabs still set up stones of witness, whenever they first catch sight of certain holy places. The stones in the circle may have been "witness" stones, or else stones at which sacrifice was made. Yet the regularity of their number, generally ten or a dozen, forbids much hopeful speculation in these lines. Another theory connects the burial circle with phallic worship; the circle itself would answer to the yoni symbol and the menhirs upon it to the linga. The principles of life and of death would thus be worshipped together, which is not an uncommon circumstance. The cup-markings so often met with on burial monuments lend additional weight to this view.

To sum up. Our negative conclusions are, that neither the Celts nor their Druids built these stone circles, nor were they for sun or fire worship, and they were not the foundation either of dwellings or of dismantled mounds. Our positive results are, that the stone circles were built by pre-historic races—in this country, probably by the Picts; that they are connected with burial, though built independent of mounds and other forms of tomb; that they are also connected with ancestor worship, and that the whole difficulty resolves itself into the question of why they are of circular form and why the stones are set at intervals.

CELTIC BURIAL.

First published by Eneas Mackay, 1917.

*First published in Transactions of the Inverness Scientific Society
and Field Club. Volume III. 1893.*

CELTIC BURIAL.

In ordinary works on archæology the term "Celtic" signifies the pre-Roman period, or, in Ireland and Northern Scotland, the pre-Christian period. Jewitt, who is typical of nearly all the other archæologists, considers the Celtic period to be co-extensive with the Stone and Bronze Ages : the Iron Age is always Roman or Saxon. "The Celt, the Roman, and the Saxon " is a work by Mr. Wright, and its title accurately represents his views as to the ethnology of our country, which he and most others regard as composed of only those three races. The Celts are usually regarded as aboriginal, and the Romans and Teutons are successive invaders. It matters not that this " Celtic " period contains the divers elements of the Stone Age, old and new, and of the Bronze Age ; nor do some archæologists seem to understand that the barrows of those ages contain proofs that two, if not more, races are included in their Celtic race. " Celtic " burial is, with holders of such theories, as varied as the ages and epochs of pre-historic times, and the only thing that can be predicated of it is that, when the bodies are unburnt, they are in a cramped posture, and there are no iron accompaniments. Pagan burial, in this country, if accompanied by iron, is non-

Celtic—so the ordinary archæologists say. Pagan burial with iron accompaniments, is Teutonic.

It is against this use of the term " Celtic " that I wish to protest. It is a wrong use of it—wrong on historical and scientific grounds. The Celts are a people perfectly well known historically ; we meet with them in ancient history from 500 B.C. downwards, and we have them still in modern times. Ancient writers describe their manners and customs with fair fulness of detail, and modern science has proved that their language belongs to the same type and is descended of the same stock as those of Greece, Rome, and Germany. A study of their manners and customs, as the ancients relate them, and as the old Irish literature reveals them, presents the same leading features of political and social organisation, the same kind of religion and of mythology, and the same kind of judicial system as were prevalent in early times in Rome and Greece. Celtic institutions are co-extensive with the use of the Celtic language, for language and culture follow each other. A Celtic language implies a Celtic culture, or stage of civilisation. A people speaking a Celtic language need not necessarily be of Celtic race or descent, but they must have Celtic institutions and culture. A Celtic race may have conquered another race, and may have imposed their own language and customs upon them. Nevertheless, it must be admitted that customs and institutions, just as words and idioms of another race, may persist in the amalgamated race ; indeed, when one Aryan race conquers another, the struggle is often long and doubtful as to which language and institutions will prevail, for both are there of a similar class. The Aryans, in contact with any other races outside the Semitic, always prevail, their language and culture being vastly superior.

Philological science has proved that the Celts belong to the Indo-European family of speech. This Indo-European or Aryan race lived together over 3000 B.C. somewhere in Middle or Eastern Europe, and nearly all the languages of Europe and the leading languages of India, past and present, including that of Persia, are descended from this ancient Aryan tongue. Descended groups situated near one another are more intimately related ; thus Latin and Celtic are more allied to each other than either of them is to any other European language, ancient or modern. Now, words represent things, actions, institutions, and if we find the same word for the same idea in Greek, Latin, and Celtic, we are certain that thing, action, or institution existed among them when they lived together. In this way we have a tolerably clear idea of the state of civilisation among the Italo-Celtic race ; and, when European history begins with Greece and Rome, the glimpses we get of Celtic history, language, and customs, indicate what might be expected *a priori* from a consideration of the kindred institutions and languages of Rome and Greece. Ancient Gaul

presents to our view the same political features as
Greece of Herodotus' time, or earlier ; the manners
and customs of Gaul remind the Greek historians
of the life in Homer's time ; and certainly the
Gaulish burial customs are described by Cæsar in
language that makes an admirable summary of
Homer's description of the burial of Patroclus and
Hector. Greek burial in the Homeric ages was as
follows :—A pyre of wood was constructed, and on
the top of it the body was laid. Sheep and oxen
were slain, their fat was placed about and upon the
body, and their carcases were heaped around it.
Jars of honey and oil were placed on the pile. Horses,
favourite dogs, and captives were slain and cast
on the pyre, and the whole set on fire. A wail
was raised, and the dead addressed by name. When
the fire burned low, it was finally extinguished with
wine, the bones were collected—" the whitened
bones," as the poet says—and placed in an urn of
gold. Then they dug a grave, and raised over it
a mound. Homer also speaks of " the pillar-stone
that standeth on the barrow of a dead man or of a
woman." In historic times, in Greece and Republican Rome, the burning of the dead was the exception,
not the rule—inhumation of the body at full length
being the ordinary method of disposal of the dead ;
but in Imperial Rome the custom revived, and
became the rule, while inhumation, at least of the
better classes, was the exception. Christianity,
however, finally stopped the burning of the dead.

The old mounds had also developed into the elegance of built tombs, vaults, and monuments with inscriptions and other accessories of civilisation.

Among the Celts of Gaul in Cæsar's time, however, the Homeric age of burial was still prevalent ; all the classic writers of that and the succeeding century testify to the burning of the bodies among the Gauls, but they are silent as to the character of the tombs. " Their funerals," Cæsar says, " are magnificent and costly, considering their civilisation ; and all that they think was dear to them when alive they put in the fire, even animals ; and shortly before this generation the slaves and dependants that they were considered to have loved were burned along with them in the regular performance of funeral rites." Diodorus, Cæsar's contemporary, says :— " For among them the opinion of Pythagoras prevails, that the souls of men are immortal, and in the course of a fixed number of years they live again, the soul entering another body. Accordingly, at the burial of the dead, some cast letters addressed to their departed relatives upon the funeral pile, under the belief that the dead will read them." Mela (first century, A.D.) confirms this fully :— " They burn and bury along with the dead whatever is of use to them when alive ; business accounts and payment of debt were passed on to the next world, and there were some who, of their own free will, cast themselves on the funeral piles of their relatives, expecting to live along with them."

Their vivid belief in a future existence is ridiculed by Valerius Maximus, a writer practically contemporary with Mela :—" Money loans are given, to be repaid in the next world, because they hold men's souls to be immortal.   I would call them fools did these trousered philosophers not have the same belief as lay under the cloak of Pythagoras." The scientific deduction which we can make from the similarity of language and general institutions among Greeks, Romans, and Celts, that Celtic burial customs were identical with those of early Greece and Rome, is amply proved from these classical quotations ; but we can also bring the light of archæology to bear on the matter. Gaulish tombs, which are tumuli with a kernel of stone present ornaments and utensils of bronze and iron, skeletons of men and animals, or cinerary urns, just such as we might expect from *a priori* reasoning and from the classical references. The Celts of Britain were in a more Homeric age than those of Gaul ; they used war chariots, armour, and equipments, and conducted war operations in a manner similar to the Homeric heroes. That the Irish were in a similar style of culture we know from their oldest writings.   We have rich remains of old Irish myth and legend.   The age of Cuchulinn, which is placed by the Irish historians at the beginning of our era, reproduces in a striking and original manner the main features of the Homeric age.   The war chariots, the feasts with their chief share and place for the champion, the warrior life and occupations, the chivalrous and non-chivalrous ideas, are all mostly the same as in Homer's time. The only thing we miss is the " well-greaved " forms of the Achæans of Homer ; for the ancient Irish did not, as far as their literature shows, wear either mail armour or helmets. In this they were like several Celtic tribes who invaded Italy, and fought against the Romans in a semi-nude condition. Hence we cannot but conclude that the Celtic races, wherever they appear, be they Gauls, Britons, or ancient Gaels, present the same general manners and customs. We may safely conclude that their burial customs were also similar to one another and to those of early Greece and Rome. We may infer that, as in Greece and Rome, inhumation existed in early historic times, that is in heroic times ; indeed, inhumation was probably the most common, and undoubtedly was the usual form among the common people. Kings and chiefs were buried magnificently in tumuli and cairns ; but the common people buried in cemeteries, if they lived in villages, and did not burn the body. Proof for this view may be got in the fact that in the old Irish literature there is not a word about cremation. Cremation could not have extensively existed among the ancient Irish, or else their literature would present the fact. We know that the early Church had, in some places on the continent, a desperate struggle against the burning of the bodies. If Christianity

had such a struggle in Ireland, record of it has been
carefully—too carefully to be true—weeded out of
Irish literature.

Here, again, we have another difference between
the ancient Irish and the heroes of the Homeric
time ; the Irish did not burn their dead. Yet we
meet with a custom mentioned by Homer ; he
speaks of the pillar-stone on the cairn of a dead man
or woman. So the Irish continually refer to building the tomb, setting up the pillar-stone, and, what
Homer does not mention, inscribing on it the name.
Before considering the literary evidence in regard
to old Gaelic-burial, let us consider how archæology
tallies with the conclusions we arrive at in regard
to Celtic burial from linguistic science and from
ancient literary documents. The Celts entered
Britain some centuries B.C., and were then in their
Iron Age. Is there any archæological trace of this
earliest Iron Age ? It must be pre-Roman and pre-
Teutonic ; so we argue on scientific grounds, in-
dependently of archæology. As a rule, archæologists refuse to believe in a Celtic Iron Age before
the Romans ; it is contrary to their prejudices,
and every effort is made to explain any remains
that may belong to it as either Roman or Saxon.
Besides, burial remains of the Celtic Iron Age are
not often met with. Dr. Joseph Anderson says in
regard to Scotland, and doubtless truly :—" The
general phenomena of the burials of the Celtic
Paganism of the Iron Age in Scotland are not dis-

closed by any recorded observations known to me.
If they exist, they exist either as phenomena of
unrecognised character, or as phenomena which are
still unobserved." In England matters are not
quite so bad as this. Celtic burials of the Iron
Age have been found, but unless a war-chariot was
along with the burial, any Iron Age burial of non-
Roman character was at once put down as Anglo-
Saxon. In Yorkshire, Mr. Stillingfleet in 1816-17
opened some Celtic barrows ; a man was found
buried with the remains of a chariot, and *placed
in the grave at full length*. Several other burials
similarly positioned were found by him. He found
two burials with chariots in them, remains of horse
trappings ; one barrow seemed to have held the
horses and chariot complete. It seems, however,
that only parts of the chariots—the wheels—and
parts of the trappings were laid in the grave.
Chariot wheels have been found four or five times.
Remains of pigs were also found, and we know that
the Gaulish Celts were great pig rearers ; indeed
the boar was the national emblem. Ten years
ago another barrow was opened at Arras, in Yorkshire, where the skeleton of a woman was found
laid at full length, with two chariot wheels, some
horse trappings, more especially the bridle-bit, and
other objects, such as a mirror made of iron. Other
Celtic burials have been found, but the ordinary
archæologist classifies them, despite of the Celtic
ornaments, whose parallels can only be found in

Ireland, as Anglo-Saxon. Canon Greenwell mentions several, and each time his predecessors, "no doubt by an oversight," as he charitably remarks, make them Anglo-Saxon. One at Borlaston, in Staffordshire, is in some respects typical of the rest ; it is described by Jewitt as Anglo-Saxon, yet the ornamentation he could only parallel from the collection of the Royal Irish Academy. The grave was seven feet long by two wide, cut in the solid sandstone rock fifteen inches deep. A deeper hollow had been excavated for the head, where the remains of the helmet were found ; the sword was extended by the right side, and in the left was a knife. " The skeleton," as Mr. Jewitt remarks, " had, as is so frequently the case in Anglo-Saxon interments, entirely disappeared." The body, in Celtic and Saxon burials both, was placed at full length on its back in a scooped-out grave ; it was in full dress, with the sword extended at the side, often with other weapons. Both the Celts and Teutons practised cremation at the same time as inhumation ; indeed, the burial customs of Celt, Roman, and Teuton, when in the same stage of culture, were exactly alike. It is no wonder that archæologists have been led astray when they stick to mere archæology.

We may pass, in the last place, to the burial customs of the ancient Irish, as recorded in their literature. There is a rich literary reference to burial, but previous to this literature we have the inscriptions of early Celtic and Christian times.

The Gaulish inscriptions show that a cairn was raised over the grave, and on this cairn a pillar-stone. One inscription in Gaulish may be given, the bilingual of Todi :—" Ategnati Druticni carnitu artvass Coisis Druticnos," for which the Latin may be given thus—" Ategnati Druti filio lapides (sepulcrales) congessit Coisis Druti filius." The Welsh inscription at Penmachno is of quite a similar kind ; it is in very barbarous Latin :—" Carausius hic jacit in hoc congeries lapidum "—" Carausius lies here in this cairn of stones." The book of Armagh, 1000 years old, records that St. Patrick, " sepelivit illum aurigam Totum calvum, id est, totmael et congregavit lapides erga sepulturam." In Adamnan's life of Columba we read that Artbranan, the old chief, who was brought to the Saint when in Skye, " believed and was baptised, and when the baptism was administered to him he died on the same spot, according to the prediction of the Saint ; and his companions buried him there, raising a heap of stones over his grave." Whitley Stokes, one of the greatest Celtic scholars now living, remarks— " I have not met with anything in Celtic literature showing that the Celts practised cremation. But the number of sepulchral urns which have been found in France, Britain, and Ireland proves that they, like the Greeks, either burned or buried the human body. They had biers, but I cannot find that they used coffins. Their *carni* or cairns (cognate with Greek *kranaos ?*) seem to have been invariably

composed of stones, and thus differed from the
Greek *tumboi*, Latin *tumuli*, which might be made
either of stones or earth."

Three features of burial constantly occur in the
Irish records : these are the grave or *fert*, which
was dug out ; a mound or cairn—*duma* or *lecht*—
was raised above the grave ; and a pillar-stone,
coirthe, or stone, *lia*, placed in or upon the mound
or cairn. Finally, an inscription was cut again
on this pillar-stone or *lia*. Similarly the *stēlē* stood
upon the *tumbos* in Homeric and Greek times generally. Keating, an Irish historian and antiquary
of the 17th century, places this form of burial as
his first. He says :—" They used to make a *fert*
in the earth corresponding in length and breadth
with the corpse ; they then deposited the corpse
therein, with the soles of the feet turned to the east,
and the crown of the head to the west ; and put a
carn of stones over it, which was called a *lecht*."
The orientation of the body, with sunward face, is
Christian, though Pagan in its ultimate origin. A
quotation or two from the MSS. will further elucidate
the point. A MS. of the 12th century, called the
Book of Leinster, tells us—relating events a dozen
centuries earlier :—" A grave was dug for Ferb,
and her stone was raised, and an inscription in Ogam
was written, and a mound (duma) was made around
the stone." Here the pillar-stone was set on the
grave, and partially covered with the mound.

Traces of the old Pagan custom of burying arms

and valuables, and even slaves along with the dead,
peep out here and there in the elder records. The
oldest Irish MS., called the Book of the Dun Cow,
dated about 1100, tells, in recording events shortly
before Christ, that Eochaid, King of Ireland, left
" Ailill at Fremain of Teffia to die. . . . and he
left Etain with Ailill, in order that she might have
his *tuigmaine* or honours made—that is, to dig his
fert, to make his *guba* (the lamentation, or keening),
and *to slay his quadrupeds."* The quadrupeds were
doubtless favourite animals, or, possibly, victims
in honour of his *manes.* A scene from the third
century may be quoted, occurring in a MS. of the
fourteenth century :—" We, the Fiann," said Cailte,
" both high and low, great and small, king and knight,
raised a loud shout of lamentation for the brave and
valiant champions. And a mound was dug for
each of them, and they were put into them, and his
own arms along with each. Their tombstones were
raised over their graves, and their Ogam names were
written then." The burial of Fothaid Airgthech
in the third century is thus described in the MS.
of 1100 :—" There is a chest of stone about him
in the earth. There are his two rings of silver, and
his two *bunne do-at* (bracelets), and his torque of
silver on his coffin, and there is a pillar-stone at his
cairn, and an Ogam is on the end of the pillar-stone,
which is in the earth, and what is on it is ' Eochaidh
Airgtheach here, who was killed by Cailte in battle,
on the side of Finn.' "

Human victims are recorded in one instance as being sacrificed. King Fiachra, in the fourth century, returned from Munster with fifty hostages, but he died of his wounds by the way, and " his grave was made, and his mound was raised, and his *cluiche cainte* (games and dirges) were instituted, and his Ogam name was written, and the hostages, which had been brought from the south, were buried alive round Fiachra's grave." Though laying the body on its back at full length was the ordinary rule, it was departed from in special cases. We know that in Christian times Charlemagne, like his Pagan predecessor, was buried seated on his throne. St. Patrick's unbelieving contemporary, King Loegaire, is recorded in the Book of Armagh to have said :— " My father, Niall, did not allow me to believe, but that I should be buried on the heights of Tara like men standing up in war." And the annotator adds :—" Because the heathen are wont to be placed armed in their tombs, with their weapons at hand, face to face, until the day *erdathe*, as the magi have it—that is the day of the judgment of the Lord." As a consequence we read in the Dun Cow MS. that the " body of King Loegaire was interred with his armour on the south-east, and outside the royal *rath* of Loegaire, at Tara, and his face to the south, against Leinster, as battling against them, for when living they were his foes." Burial of arms, as in the foregoing case, is mentioned very often ; an old " Druidic " poem celebrates the fall of Mog-

Neid, King of Munster in the second century of our
era ; it says—

> " The grave of Mog-Neid is on Magh Tualaing,
> With his lance at his shoulder,
> With his club, so rapid in action,
> With his helmet, with his sword."

King Dathi, in the fifth century, was buried—
according to his wish—with his red javelin in his
hand in the grave, and his grave facing the Ulstermen, and his face turned towards them. And so
long as his face was towards the Ulstermen they
were defeated, and it was not until they turned
Dathi's face mouth downward that they could
conquer his people. We thus infer that warriors,
at least great warriors, were buried with their faces
to their foes, and sometimes standing straight up.
In Welsh mythology the head of King Bran was
buried facing France, and prophecy said that so
long as it was there and facing so, no invasion could
be successful. But Arthur, in his self-confidence,
exhumed the head of Bran, feeling capable of de-
fending his country without such aid. But, alas !
his successors failed, and the Britons lost their
kingdom.

The heroic tales and ballads of the Scottish Gael,
though taken down from oral recitation since Macpherson's time, yet contain valuable and authentic
references to ancient customs. In the story of the
death of the demi-god Cuchulinn, his foster-father,
Conall, is represented as having sworn that whosoever

told him of Cuchulinn's death should that instant be slain. Cuchulinn's charioteer, who knew of this, tells the fact of his master's death in a roundabout way. " Well, Loegaire," says Conall, " how is my dear friend Cuchullinn ? " " He is well," said Loegaire. " He is at present after making for himself a new house." " What house has he made ? Would not his ancestral house do for him ? " " It is a house in the new fashion." " What is the new fashion that he has discovered ? " " O, it is only a little house. When he lays him down straight on his back on the floor, and he stretches his legs, his soles touch the one end and his head the other end of the house, and the point of his nose touches the rooftree." " That is the same," said Conall, " as if you said that Cuchulinn is dead." " I have not told of Cuchulinn's death ; I call you as witness to that." " Quite right, my lad, etc." Another version just lately recovered in the Isles adds a very graphic touch : " Cuchulinn has a new house, with his head reaching the spars and the big sword on his breast." The " Lay of the Heads," which ends the story of Cuchulinn's death, purports to be a dialogue between Emer, Cuchulinn's wife, and Conall, when the latter tells the names of the heroes he has slain in revenge for the Cu or Hound, that is Cuchulinn. Finally Emer says :—

> " Conall it is time for us
> Cuchulinn in the earth to lay ;
> Let us finish the digging of his grave—
> His narrow hard bed of stone.

. . . . . .

' And, Conall, I shall go into the grave,
For weak is my strength as I am ;
Place my mouth 'gainst mouth of Cu,
For meet it is I should with him go.''

A similar request to that of Emer's—the laying her in the grave beside her love, and mouth to mouth— is made by three other heroines of Gaelic tragic story. Deirdre requests to be laid beside Naois, while the three hounds and the three shields of the three heroic brothers are also to be put in the grave, and their three swords above them. Similarly Grainne wishes to be buried with Diarmid, while Dargo's wife expressed her love for her husband when the connected story of his death was brought to her, the effects of which killed her, in these words—

" Chi mi 'n seobhag, chi mi 'n cù
Leis an d'roinn mo rùn an t-sealg,
'S o na b'ionmhuinn leis an triuir,
Càirear sinn 'san ùir le Dearg.''

I see the hawk, I see the hound,
With which my love performed the chase,
And as the three to him were bound,
Let us in earth with Dearg have place.

The conclusion to which we come is that the Celts, when they practised inhumation, as they universally did in the British Isles immediately before Christianity was introduced, buried their dead at full length, generally placing some weapons by or upon the body, and not rarely killing favourite animals and burying them along with their master. The grave was called in old Gaelic a *fert*, and it was dug ; then a mound

was raised over it, and after the introduction of
Ogam writing, a pillar-stone was placed in or on
the mound with the person's name in Ogams.   There
is no mention of any coffin, but the " Lay of the
Heads " evidently points to the body being at
times boxed in with stones.   One thing appears
to be certain : the small box graves, three feet by
two, made of flagstones, where the body is cramped
up—knees to chin, and lying on its side as a rule,
are not " Celtic " graves at all.   They do not suit
the literary references to burial among the Gael,
nor do they correspond with the finds in Celtic
tumuli in France and Britain.   These burials must
therefore be attributed to the earlier race or races
which the Celts found in these islands when they
first came here from mid Europe.